David Self has been a freelance writer and broadcaster for 30 years, specializing in literary, media and religious topics. He has published books on the problem of suffering, the world faiths and his most recent title is *The Lion Treasury of Saints*. He is a winner of the Sandford St Martin Prize for religious broadcasting and a communicant member of the Church of England. He lives in the Cambridgeshire Fens.

Somebody Once Said

An Anthology of Quotations
for Preachers and Speakers

Compiled by David Self

First published in Great Britain in 2003 by
Society for Promoting Christian Knowledge
Holy Trinity Church
Marylebone Road
London NW1 4DU

British Library Cataloguing-in-Publication Data
A catalogue record for this book is available from the British
Library

ISBN 0-281-05565-3

1 3 5 7 9 10 8 6 4 2

Typeset by FiSH Books, London
Printed in Great Britain by Bookmarque Ltd, Croydon, Surrey

~ Contents ~

~ Introduction ~

It was only a casual remark but it resulted in the largest number of letters I have ever received after one broadcast. In the course of that particular radio programme, I happened to say that one of the things that annoyed me most about church services was a preacher who began by saying, 'Somebody once said...'

Why, I pondered on air, couldn't they be bothered to look up the source of their quotation?

Half my letters came from listeners who agreed with me. The other half came from preachers pointing out they didn't have access to suitable dictionaries of quotations and, anyway, they didn't have time to hunt around a library. This small book is therefore intended to help such preachers to trace some of their favourite sayings and to find new sources of inspiration or starting points; and, at the same time, to provide other readers with food for thought or meditation – or even parish magazine editors with copy!

This is an anthology, not a dictionary. Obviously no book of this size could claim to be comprehensive and, inevitably, it is a subjective selection. Omissions may be due to editorial ignorance or preference. My principal criterion as to what makes an apt or helpful quotation has been (in the words of Egon J. Beaudoin, a man whose name seemingly exists only within dictionaries of quotations) 'Something that somebody said that seemed to make sense at the time.'

I have excluded quotations from the Bible, the Book of Common Prayer and from hymns, which can be found in profusion in many other books. By and large, I have also excluded quotations from the poets, preferring to concentrate on the prosaic, the matter-of-fact and the direct. I have also tended to exclude lengthier quotations, in the hope that what is included will be the more easily memorable.

Because it is an anthology and not a dictionary, I have chosen to present the quotations thematically rather than chronologically or biographically. This is partly to encourage browsing and even meditation on a given theme; and to help speakers and preachers locate an appropriate quotation for their chosen subject.

I certainly do not endorse every entry. Several are included as 'provocations', to stimulate thought and even disagreement. Because of this, some of their authors no doubt would have been surprised (even annoyed) to find themselves in a 'Christian' anthology.

And because it is a subjective anthology, I make no apology if a reader's favourite quotation has been omitted (though I should be pleased to hear of likely candidates for inclusion: contact me at david.self@virgin.net) but I do offer two apologies. First, despite my best efforts to double-check every entry, I realize there may well be a misquotation somewhere or other. To that end I can only repeat one Ambrose Bierce's definition of quoting: 'The act of repeating erroneously the words of another' (in *The Devil's Dictionary*, 1911).

Second, I am somewhat embarrassed by the number of times in which the male pronoun (or the word 'man') appears to the apparent exclusion of half the human race. Such was the custom of previous centuries but, *pace* Ambrose Bierce, I have not considered it my job to alter or to censor what 'somebody once said' in the interests of modern sensibilities.

A brief biographical note on Ambrose Bierce, along with details of all the authors quoted (where known), will be found in the Author Index at the back of this book. Further information would be welcome.

David Self
Fenland, 2003

~ Unbelief ~

Religion ... is the opium of the people. *Karl Marx*

Unbelief is blind. *John Milton*

It's an interesting view of atheism, as a sort of crutch for those who can't stand the reality of God. *Tom Stoppard in his play* Jumpers

In my experience, modern atheists are the most awful killjoys God ever invented ... These days, atheists are Against God because they know that lots of people get a buzz, a kick, a nice warm glow from religion and that annoys them because they're mean and uptight. These people also tend not to have pets. *Julie Burchill in the* Guardian Weekend *magazine (2002)*

An atheist is a man without any invisible means of support. *John Buchan*

An atheist is a man who believes himself an accident. *Francis Thompson*

Atheism is rather in the lip than in the heart of man. *Francis Bacon*

Some are atheists only in fair weather. *Thomas Fuller*

The agnostic's prayer: 'O God, if there is a god, save my soul, if I have a soul.' *Joseph Ernest Renan*

Atheism shows a strength of mind, but only to a certain degree. *Blaise Pascal*

Many things are not believed because their current explanation is not believed. *Friedrich Wilhelm Nietzsche*

If only God would give me some clear sign! Like making a large deposit in my name at a Swiss bank. *Woody Allen*

Have you ever seen a room from which faith has gone? ... Like a marriage from which love has gone ... And patience, patience everywhere like a fog. *Graham Greene*

Someone asked [the famous atheist] Bertrand Russell at some meeting, 'Lord Russell, what will you say when you die and are brought face to face with your maker?' He replied without hesitation: 'God,' I shall say, 'why did you make the evidence for your existence so insufficient?' *Told by another atheist, A. J. Ayer, in the London* Evening Standard

The atheist who is moved by love is moved by the spirit of God; an atheist who lives by love is saved by his faith in the God whose existence (under that name) he denies. *William Temple*

Those who do not believe have one thing in common with those who do believe – namely that the Lord believes in them. *Helder Camara*

They that deny a God destroy man's nobility. *Francis Bacon*

The writers against religion, whilst they oppose every system, are wisely careful never to set up any of their own. *Edmund Burke*

[Defining a cynic:] A man who knows the price of everything and the value of nothing. *Oscar Wilde*

The optimist proclaims that we live in the best of all possible worlds; and the pessimist fears that this is true. *James Branch Cabell*

He that seeks trouble never misses. *George Herbert*

Ten thousand difficulties do not make one doubt. *John Henry Newman*

He is a dull man who is always sure. *Henry L. Mencken*

Prejudice, not being founded on reason, cannot be removed by argument. *Samuel Johnson*

It is never too late to give up your prejudices. *Henry David Thoreau*

Fear is nothing but sin. *George Herbert*

The only thing we have to fear is fear itself. *Franklin D. Roosevelt*

After coming into contact with a religious man, I always feel that I must wash my hands. *Friedrich Wilhelm Nietzsche*

~ Belief ~

What is faith unless it is to believe what you do not see? *St Augustine of Hippo*

Religions die when they are proved to be true. *Oscar Wilde*

Faith may be defined briefly as an illogical belief in the occurrence of the improbable. *Henry L. Mencken*

Faith keeps many doubts in her pay. If I could not doubt, I should not believe. *Henry David Thoreau*

It takes application and a kind of genius to believe anything. *T. S. Eliot*

Let us weigh the gain and the loss, in wagering that God is. Consider these alternatives: if you win, you win all; if you lose, you lose nothing. Do not hesitate then, to wager that he is. *Blaise Pascal's famous wager that it is a better bet to bet on the existence of God rather than on his non-existence.*

A religion without mystery must be a religion without God. *Jeremy Taylor*

The first idea of religion arose, not from a contemplation of the works of nature, but from a concern with regard to the events of life. *David Hume*

Do not seek to understand in order that you may believe, but believe, so that you may understand. *St Augustine of Hippo*

Scepticism is the beginning of faith. *Oscar Wilde*

Religion is caught, not taught. *William Ralph Inge*

Faith is a gift which can be given or withdrawn; it is something infused into us, not produced by us. *Robert H. Benson*

There are three roads to belief: reason, habit, revelation. *Blaise Pascal*

The laugh that children are born with lasts just as long as they have perfect faith. *J. M. Barrie*

It is cynicism and fear that freeze life; it is faith that thaws it out. *Harry Emerson Fosdick*

If a man believes and knows God, he can no longer ask, 'What is the meaning of my life?' *Karl Barth*

You never know how much you really believe anything until its truth or falsehood becomes a matter of life or death to you. *C. S. Lewis*

Man is what he believes. *Anton Chekhov*

What is the mark of a Christian? Faith working by love. *St Basil the Great*

All things are possible to one who believes. *St Bernard of Clairvaux*

I do not want merely to possess a faith; I want a faith that possesses me. *Charles Kingsley*

Religion is a way of walking, not a way of talking. *William Ralph Inge*

Science without religion is lame, religion without science is blind. *Albert Einstein*

Faith is never identical with piety. *Karl Barth*

Faith is much better than belief. Belief is when someone else does the thinking. *R. Buckminster Fuller*

It is certainly no part of religion to compel religion. *Quintus Tertullian*

It is as absurd to argue men, as to torture them, into believing. *John Henry Newman*

Never, for the sake of peace and quiet, deny your own experience or convictions. *Dag Hammarskjöld*

There is only one religion, though there are a hundred versions of it. *George Bernard Shaw*

Creeds are devices to keep heretics out rather than draw people in. *Gerald Priestland*

It is the test of a good religion whether you can make a joke about it. *G. K. Chesterton*

My dear child, you must believe in God in spite of what the clergy tell you. *Benjamin Jowett*

Ultimately, faith is the only key to the universe. *Thomas Merton*

~ God ~

The Nature of God

God is a sea of infinite substance. *St John of Damascus (his is the most frequently quoted definition of God during the Middle Ages)*

God is that than which nothing greater can be conceived. *Anselm of Canterbury*

If God did not exist, it would be necessary to invent him. *Voltaire*

God can stand being told by [atheists such as] Professor Ayer and Marghanita Laski that he doesn't exist. *J. B. Priestley in the magazine* The Listener *1965*

God and all the attributes of God are eternal. *Benedict de Spinoza*

God has many names though he is only one being. *Aristotle*

God is an infinite circle whose centre is everywhere and whose circumference is nowhere. *St Augustine of Hippo*

God is invisible, though he is seen; incomprehensible, though manifested by grace; inconceivable, though conceived by human senses. *Quintus Tertullian*

If God is 'always greater' then there can be no limit to what is known about God. *Michael Barnes*

God is called omnipotent because he can do all things that are possible absolutely. *St Thomas Aquinas*

God's omnipotence means power to do all that is intrinsically possible, not to do the intrinsically impossible. You may attribute miracles to him, but not nonsense. *C. S. Lewis*

Speculations over God and the world are almost always idle, the thoughts of idlers, spectators of the theatre of life. 'Is there a God?' 'Has man a soul?' 'Why must we die?' 'How many hairs has the devil's grandmother?' 'When is the day of judgement?' – all these are idle questions, and one fool can ask more of them than a hundred wise men can answer. *Eugen Rosenstock-Huessy*

It is the final proof of God's omnipotence that he need not exist in order to save us. *Peter de Vries*

I imagine when it comes to the next prayer book they won't write He, meaning Him with a capital h. God will be written in the lower case to banish any lurking sense of inferiority his worshippers might feel. *Alan Bennett in his 1978 play* The Old Country

I have never understood why it should be considered derogatory to the Creator to suppose that he has a sense of humour. *William Ralph Inge*

The finger of God never leaves identical fingerprints. *Stanislaw Lec*

It is a mistake to suppose that God is only, or even chiefly, concerned with religion. *William Temple*

The almighty has his own purposes. *Abraham Lincoln*

We cannot study God. *Michael Barnes*

Where truth is, there is God. *Cervantes*

Where there is peace, God is. *George Herbert*

Our Father

Is man one of God's blunders or is God one of man's? *Friedrich Wilhelm Nietzsche*

God can no more do without us than we can do without him. *Meister Eckhart*

We could not seek God unless he were seeking us. *Thomas Merton*

It is easy to know God so long as you do not tax yourself with defining him. *Joseph Joubert*

It is the heart that experiences God and not the reason. *Blaise Pascal*

By faith we know his existence; in glory we shall know his nature. *Blaise Pascal*

God forces no one, for love cannot compel, and God's service, therefore, is a thing of perfect freedom. *Hans Denck*

To love God is something greater than to know him. *St Thomas Aquinas*

To be alive to the reality of God is to be aware of his glorious foolishness. *John Austin Baker*

God is the great listener. *Michael Hollings*

The soul that is united with God is feared by the devil as though it were God himself. *St John of the Cross*

We must fear God through love, not love him through fear. *Jean Pierre Camus*

The hardness of God is kinder than the softness of men. *C. S. Lewis*

God is a kind Father. He sets us all in the places where he wishes us to be employed; and that employment is truly 'Our Father's business'. *John Ruskin*

The God to whom little boys say their prayers has a face very like their mother's. *James M. Barrie*

If we address him as children, it is because he tells us he is our Father. If we unbosom ourselves to him as a friend, it is because he calls us friends. *William Cowper*

Never let fear create the God of childhood; fear is the creation of a wicked spirit; shall the devil become the grandfather of God? *Johann Paul Richter*

Almighty God influences us and works in us, through our minds, not without them or in spite of them. *John Henry Newman*

Man proposes but God disposes. *Thomas à Kempis*

God does not comfort us to make us comfortable, but to make us comforters. *John Henry Jowett*

The more we depend on God, the more dependable we find he is. *Cliff Richard*

I have held many things in my hands, and I have lost them all; but whatever I have placed in God's hands, that I still possess. *Corrie ten Boom*

God is not a cosmic bell-boy for whom we can press a button to get things. *Harry Emerson Fosdick*

There is nothing that God cannot accomplish. *Marcus Tullius Cicero*

I'm glad now that I discovered God before I discovered the Bible. *Richard Holloway*

We expect too much of God, but he always seems ready. *John F. Kennedy*

Put your trust in God but keep your powder dry. *Oliver Cromwell*

A man with God is always in the majority. *John Knox*

In his will is our peace. *Dante Alighieri*

~ Jesus Christ ~

At the name of Jesus, every voice goes plummy. *Dorothy L. Sayers*

Whether you think Jesus was God or not, you must admit he was a first-rate political economist. *George Bernard Shaw in a preface 'Jesus as Economist'*

If Jesus Christ were to come today people would not even crucify him. They would ask him to dinner, and hear what he has to say, and make fun of it. *Thomas Carlyle*

They should have known that he [Jesus Christ] was God. His patience should have proved that to them. *Quintus Tertullian*

'Gentle Jesus, meek and mild' is a snivelling modern invention with no warrant in the Gospels. *George Bernard Shaw*

The one and only thing that seems to have roused the 'meek and mild' Son of God to a display of outright physical violence was precisely the assumption that 'business is business'. *Dorothy L. Sayers*

No one ever made more trouble than the 'gentle Jesus meek and mild'. *James M. Gillis*

Nobody worries about Christ as long as he can be shut up in churches. He is quite safe inside. But there is always trouble if you try and let him out. *G. A. Studdert-Kennedy*

Christ the tiger. *T. S. Eliot*

Jesus had flair. *Colin Morris*

Jesus of Nazareth was the most scientific man that ever trod the globe. He plunged beneath the material surface of things, and found the spiritual cause. *Mary Baker Eddy*

When Christ came into the world, peace was sung; and when he went out of the world, peace was bequeathed. *Francis Bacon*

Christ has turned all our sunsets into dawns. *St Clement of Alexandria*

Light, even though it passes through pollution, is not polluted. *St Augustine of Hippo*

Life is filled with meaning as soon as Jesus Christ enters it. *Stephen Neill*

Christ is not valued at all unless he is valued above all. *St Augustine of Hippo*

Jesus Christ will be Lord of all or he will not be Lord at all. *St Augustine of Hippo*

Verbally in Scripture, visually in sacrament, Jesus Christ is set forth as the only Saviour of sinners. *John Stott*

If Jesus isn't the lord of your life someone else will be. *Donald Coggan*

If Christ is with us, who is against us? *St Bernard of Clairvaux*

If you are looking for the way by which you should go, take Christ, for he is himself the way. *St Thomas Aquinas*

Jesus does not give recipes that show the way to God as other teachers of religion do. He is himself the way. *Karl Barth*

It is easy to want things from the Lord himself, as though the gift could ever be preferable to the Giver. *St Augustine of Hippo*

If Jesus Christ is not true God, how could he help us? If he is not true man, how could he help us? *Dietrich Bonhoeffer*

I believe there is no one lovelier, deeper, more sympathetic and more perfect than Jesus. *Fyodor Dostoyevsky*

Christianity is a person, one who loved us so much, one who calls for our love. Christianity is Christ. *Oscar Romero*

In Jesus the service of God and the service of the least of the brethren were one. *Dietrich Bonhoeffer*

Christ did not love humanity. He never said that he loved humanity. He loved men. *G. K. Chesterton*

Christ's love is a love without angles, a love that asks nothing in return. *David Wilkerson*

What other people think of me is becoming less and less important; what they think of Jesus because of me is critical. *Cliff Richard*

Keep close to Jesus. *Paul the Great*

To be like Christ is to be a Christian. *William Penn*

~ The Holy Spirit ~

Three in one, one in three, perfectly straightforward. Any doubts about that see your maths master. *Schoolmaster to a boy in Alan Bennett's play* Forty Years On

How many clergy, as Trinity Sunday draws near, groan within themselves at the thought that it will be their duty to try to expound this dry and abstract doctrine to congregations for whom they anticipate it will have but little interest? *Leonard Hodgson*

The Holy Spirit ... writes his own gospel and he writes it in the hearts of the faithful. *Jean Pierre de Caussade*

Every time we say, 'I believe in the Holy Spirit', we mean that we believe there is a living God able and willing to enter human personality and change it. *J. B. Phillips*

Those who have the gale of the Holy Spirit go forward even in sleep. *Brother Lawrence*

I should as soon attempt to raise flowers if there were no atmosphere, or produce fruits if there were neither light nor heat, as to regenerate men if I did not believe there was a Holy Ghost. *Henry Ward Beecher*

Grace is not sought nor bought nor wrought. It is a free gift of the Almighty God. *Billy Graham*

Happy the man whose words come from the Holy Spirit and not from himself. *St Antony of Padua*

When the Holy Spirit enters the heart of man, he shows him all his inner poverty and weakness. *Innocent Veniaminov*

The gift of the Holy Ghost closes the last gap between the life of God and ours. *Austin Farrer*

Both in heaven and on earth the Lord is made known only by the Holy Spirit, and not through ordinary learning. *Staretz Silouan*

The Holy Spirit teaches prayer. No one, until he receives the Spirit, can pray in a manner truly pleasing to God. *Innocent Veniaminov*

The man who has the Holy Spirit within him, in however slight a degree, sorrows day and night for all mankind. *Staretz Silouan*

The Spirit of God first imparts love; he next inspires hope, and then gives liberty. *Dwight L. Moody*

Where the Spirit of the Lord is, there is love for enemies and prayer for the whole world. *Staretz Silouan*

When Christians ... take counsel together, their purpose ... should not be to ascertain the mind of the majority, but what is the mind of the Holy Spirit – something which may be quite different. *Margaret Thatcher*

Before Christ sent the church into the world he sent the Spirit into the church. The same order must be observed today. *John Stott*

~ Creation ~

To create is to bring a thing into existence without any previous material at all to work on. *St Thomas Aquinas*

In the beginning God fashioned Adam, not because he had need of human beings, but so that he might have beings on whom to bestow his benefits. *Irenaeus*

You have made us for yourself, and our heart is restless till it finds rest in you. *St Augustine of Hippo*

The universe is but one vast symbol of God. *Thomas Carlyle*

The universe is like a safe to which there is a combination. But the combination is locked up in the safe. *Peter de Vries*

That the universe was formed by a fortuitous concourse of atoms, I will no more believe than that the accidental jumbling of the alphabet would fall into a most ingenious treatise of philosophy. *Jonathan Swift*

What is now proved was once only imagined. *William Blake*

Science has promised us truth ... It has never promised us either peace or happiness. *Gustave Le Bon*

We can in fact get at the Creator only through the world. *Thomas Corbishley*

You will find something far greater in the woods than you will in books. Stones and trees will teach you what you can never learn from masters. *St Bernard of Clairvaux*

If created things are so utterly lovely, how gloriously beautiful must he be who made them! *Antony of Padua*

Love all God's creation, the whole of it and every grain of sand in it. Love every leaf, every ray of God's light. Love the animals, love the plants, love everything. If you love everything, you will perceive the divine mystery in things. Once you have perceived it, you will begin to comprehend it better every day, and you will come at last to love the world with an all-embracing love. *Fyodor Dostoyevsky*

God passes through the thicket of the world, and wherever his glance falls he turns all things to beauty. *St John of the Cross*

Nature is but a name for an effect whose cause is God. *William Cowper*

Every creature is a divine word because it proclaims God. *St Bonaventure*

Nothing in all creation is so like God as stillness. *Meister Eckhart*

The reason why God's servants love creatures so much is that they see how much Christ loves them. *St Catherine of Siena*

It is God's will that everything he has made should offer him glory. *John of Carpathos*

Natural reason is a good tree that God has planted in us; the fruits that spring from it cannot but be good. *St Francis de Sales*

Everything is good when it leaves the hand of the Creator, everything degenerates in the hand of man. *Jean Jacques Rousseau*

I see the marks of God in the heavens and the earth, but how much more in a liberal intellect, in magnanimity, in unconquerable rectitude, in a philanthropy that forgives every wrong, and that never despairs of the cause of Christ and human virtue! *William Ellery Channing*

The world will never starve for wonder; only for want of wonder. *G. K. Chesterton*

I believe there is life on other planets with principalities and sovereignties, perhaps different from us, but all a part of God's universe. *Billy Graham*

We are not our own, any more than what we possess is our own... We are God's property by creation, by redemption, by regeneration. *John Henry Newman*

Nature has some perfections to show that she is the image of God, and some defects to show that she is only his image. *Blaise Pascal*

There is no such thing as bad weather. All weather is good because it is God's. *St Teresa of Avila*

God made the country and man made the town. *William Cowper*

The planet is going to the buffers much faster than people realize. *John Oliver*

Do you create or do you destroy? *Dag Hammarskjöld*

All is for the best in the best of all possible worlds. *Voltaire*

Now let us do something beautiful for God. *Mother Teresa*

~ Scripture ~

If a man's Bible is coming apart, it is an indication that he himself is fairly well put together. *James Jennings*

When you have read the Bible, you will know it is the word of God, because you will have found it the key to your own heart, your own happiness and your own duty. *Woodrow Wilson*

I have found in the Bible words for my inmost thoughts, songs for my joy, utterance for my hidden griefs and pleadings for my shame and feebleness. *Samuel Taylor Coleridge*

A thorough knowledge of the Bible is worth more than a college education. *Theodore Roosevelt*

The Bible was written for a man with a head upon his shoulders. *Martin Luther*

Holy scripture is a stream of running water, where alike the elephant may swim, and the lamb may walk without losing its feet. *Pope St Gregory I*

Divine Scripture is the feast of wisdom, and the single books are the various dishes. *St Ambrose*

It is not possible ever to exhaust the mind of the Scriptures. It is a well that hath no bottom. *St John Chrysostom*

As in Paradise, God walks in the Holy Scriptures, seeking man. *St Ambrose*

To be ignorant of the Scripture is not to know Christ. *St Jerome*

The word of God is in the Bible as the soul is in the body. *P. T. Forsyth*

The Bible is alive, it speaks to me; it has feet, it runs after me; it has hands, it lays hold on me. *Martin Luther*

The Bible tells us to love our neighbours, and also to love our enemies; probably because they are generally the same people. *G. K. Chesterton*

The Bible without the Holy Spirit is a sundial by moonlight. *Dwight L. Moody*

In the Old Testament the New lies hidden; in the New Testament the Old is laid open. *St Augustine of Hippo*

The Gospel

It's the heart of the gospel – that nothing and nobody can fall outside the love of God. *Joyce Grenfell*

The gospel was not good advice but good news. *William Ralph Inge*

The gospel is neither a discussion or a debate. It is an announcement. *Paul S. Rees*

God writes the gospel not in the Bible alone, but on trees, and flowers, and clouds, and stars. *Martin Luther*

How could twelve uneducated men, who lived on lakes and rivers and deserts, conceive of such a great enterprise? Their preaching was clearly divinely inspired. *St John Chrysostom*

You cannot criticize the New Testament. It criticizes you. *John Jay Chapman*

Our reading of the gospel story can be and should be an act of personal communion with the living Lord. *William Temple*

[St John's Gospel] is God's love letter to the world. *Henry Ward Beecher*

Everything that we read in the sacred books shines and glitters even in the outer shell, but the marrow is sweeter. He who wants to eat the kernel must first crack the shell. *St Jerome*

Christians often forget that words are like thin planks cast over a deep chasm; if you run over quickly you are all right, but if you jump on them you fall in. *John Lawrence in* The Hard Facts of Unity

Christianity can be condensed into four words: admit, submit, commit and transmit. *Samuel Wilberforce*

To live by the law of Christ and accept him in our hearts is to turn a giant floodlight of hope into our valleys of trouble. *Charles R. Hembree*

Do not weary of reading the commandments of the Lord, and you will be adequately instructed by them. *St Bernard of Clairvaux*

Cry the gospel with your whole life. *Charles de Foucauld*

If the Sermon on the Mount is the précis of all Christian doctrine, the eight beatitudes are the précis of the whole of the Sermon on the Mount. *Jacques Bénigne Bossuet*

I should not be a Christian but for the miracles. *St Augustine of Hippo*

It is impossible on reasonable grounds to disbelieve miracles. *Blaise Pascal*

The essential fact of Christianity is that God thought all men worth the sacrifice of his Son. *William Barclay*

The gospel will not ever tell us we are innocent, but it will tell us we are loved. *Rowan Williams*

I am pleased for my brothers to study the scriptures as long as they do not neglect application to prayer. *St Francis of Assisi*

~ The Christian Life ~

Life is rather like opening a tin of sardines. We are all of us looking for the key. *Alan Bennett in his spoof sermon from the 1960s revue* Beyond the Fringe

Know that even when you are in the kitchen, our Lord moves among the pots and pans. *St Teresa of Avila*

If a man cannot be a Christian where he is, he cannot be a Christian anywhere. *Henry Ward Beecher*

I am sorry God that I forgot my prayers but remembered my breakfast. *Samuel Johnson*

Believe in Christ, and do your duty in that state of life to which God has called you. *Martin Luther*

God never imposes a duty without giving time to do it. *John Ruskin*

O Lord, may I be directed what to do and what to leave undone. *Elizabeth Fry*

God only asks you to do your best. *Robert H. Benson*

To wish to act like angels while we are still in this world is nothing but folly. *St Teresa of Avila*

Let everything be done in moderation. *St Benedict*

It is possible to be so active in the service of Christ as to forget to love him. *P. T. Forsyth*

Three things are necessary for the salvation of man: to know what he ought to believe; to know what he ought to desire; and to know what he ought to do. *St Thomas Aquinas*

I believe in one God and no more, and I hope for happiness beyond this life. I believe in the equality of man; and I believe that religious duties consist in doing justice, loving mercy, and endeavouring to make our fellow-creatures happy. *Thomas Paine*

Take short views, hope for the best, and trust in God. *Sydney Smith*

Relying on God has to begin all over again every day as if nothing had yet been done. *C. S. Lewis*

I will go anywhere provided it is forward. *David Livingstone*

If God has called you, do not spend time looking over your shoulder to see who is following you. *Corrie ten Boom*

My great concern is not whether God is on our side; my great concern is to be on God's side. *Abraham Lincoln*

The supreme object of life is neither to perfect the soul nor to enjoy God, but so to finish the work given us to do as to justify and glorify him for ever. And our quest must be by what life or death we should glorify God. *P. T. Forsyth in* Faith, Freedom and the Future

The Christian ideal has not been tried and found wanting. It has been found difficult and left untried. *G. K. Chesterton*

We must wait for God, long, meekly, in the wind and the wet, in the thunder and lightning, in the cold and the dark. Wait and he will come. *Frederick W. Faber*

Being a Christian is more than just an instantaneous conversion – it is a daily process whereby you grow to be more and more like Christ. *Billy Graham*

Christianity is like electricity. It cannot enter a person unless it can pass through. *Richard C. Raines*

Let your religion be less of a theory and more of a love affair. *G. K. Chesterton*

Keep your heart in peace; let nothing in this world disturb it; everything has an end. *St John of the Cross*

Where there is charity and wisdom, there is neither fear nor ignorance. Where there is patience and humility, there is neither anger nor vexation. Where there is poverty and joy, there is neither greed nor avarice. Where there is peace and meditation, there is neither anxiety nor doubt. *St Francis of Assisi*

Your foolish fears about the future come from the devil. Think only of the present, abandon the future to Providence. It is the good use of the present that assures the future. *Jean Pierre de Caussade*

A true Christian is a man who never for a moment forgets what God has done for him in Christ. *John Baillie*

Be to the world a sign that while we as Christians do not have all the answers, we do know and care about the questions. *Billy Graham*

When I hear somebody sigh, 'Life is hard', I am always tempted to ask 'Compared to what?' *Sydney J. Harris*

The world would use us just as it did the martyrs, if we loved God as they did. *Thomas Wilson*

A Christian is someone who shares the sufferings of God in the world. *Dietrich Bonhoeffer*

We do the works, but God works in us the doing of the works. *St Augustine of Hippo*

A Christian is an oak flourishing in winter. *Thomas Traherne*

Those who want the fewest things are closest to the gods. *Socrates quoted by the second-century writer Diogenes Laertius in his* Lives of the Greek Philosophers. *More correctly, Socrates' words should be translated as* Having the fewest wants, I am nearest to the gods.

Make a virtue of necessity. *Brother Lawrence*

Don't worry about what you do not understand . . . Worry about what you do understand in the Bible but do not live by. *Corrie ten Boom*

Most people really believe that the Christian commandments (e.g. to love one's neighbour as oneself) are intentionally a little too severe – like putting the clock ahead half an hour to make sure of not being late in the morning. *Søren Kierkegaard*

See how these Christians love one another. *Quintus Tertullian, quoting sarcastic enemies of Christianity*

Love your enemies, for they tell you your faults. *Benjamin Franklin*

Would to God we had behaved ourselves well in this world, even for one day. *Thomas à Kempis*

If you were arrested for being a Christian, would there be enough evidence to convict you? *David Otis Fuller*

Grace is indeed required to turn a man into a saint; and he who doubts this does not know what either a man or a saint is. *Blaise Pascal*

How glorious it is – and also how painful – to be an exception. *Alfred de Musset*

~ The Christian Year ~

In his life Christ is an example, showing us how to live. In his death he is a sacrifice, satisfying for our sins; in his resurrection, a conqueror; in his ascension, a king; in his intercession, a high priest. *Martin Luther*

Christmas and Epiphany

At Christmas play and make good cheer – for Christmas comes but once a year! *A Hundred Points of Good Husbandry (1557)*

I have often thought, said Sir Roger, it happens very well that Christmas should fall out in the middle of winter. *Joseph Addison (Sir Roger de Coverley was a fictional 'gentleman of Worcester-shire' who figured in some of Addison's essays in the* Spectator*)*

I really meant to think about Jesus in the run-up to Christmas but with so much going on I forgot. *Julie Burchill in the* Guardian Weekend *magazine (2003)*

He built himself a temple, a body, that is, in the Virgin, and so made himself an instrument in which to dwell. *St Athanasius*

The incarnation is the most stupendous event that can ever take place on earth. *John Henry Newman*

The fact of Jesus' coming is the final and unanswerable proof that God cares. *William Barclay*

Our Lord says to every living soul, 'I became a man for you. If you do not become God for me, you do me wrong.' *Meister Eckhart*

The ox and the ass understood more of the first Christmas than the high priests in Jerusalem. And it is the same today. *Thomas Merton*

We must not have Christ Jesus, the Lord of Life, put any more in the stable amongst the horses and asses, but he must now have the best chamber. *George Fox*

This is the festival which makes us know, indeed, that we are members of one body; it binds together the life of Christ on earth with his life in heaven; it assures us that Christmas Day belongs not to time but to eternity. *Frederick Denison Maurice*

He became what we are that he might make us what he is. *St Athanasius*

God clothed himself in vile man's flesh so he might be weak enough to suffer woe. *John Donne*

Nobody but a god can pass unscathed through the searching ordeal of incarnation. *Dorothy L. Sayers*

In order that the body of Christ might be shown to be a real body, he was born of a woman; but in order that his Godhead might be made clear he was born of a virgin. *St Thomas Aquinas*

The incarnation would be equally a miracle however Jesus entered the world. *P. T. Forsyth*

It is good to be children sometimes, and never better than at Christmas, when its mighty Founder was a child himself. *Charles Dickens*

Christmas won't be Christmas without any presents. *Louisa M. Alcott in her novel* Little Women

The Christian should resemble a fruit tree, not a Christmas tree! For the gaudy decorations of a Christmas tree are only tied on, whereas fruit grows on a fruit tree. *John Stott*

The magi worshipped this body even when it lay in a manger ... let us imitate these foreigners. *St John Chrysostom*

Passiontide

Everyone who accepts God in Christ accepts him through the cross. *Pope John Paul II*

God was executed by people painfully like us, in a society very similar to our own ... by a corrupt church, a timid politician, and a fickle proletariat led by professional agitators. *Dorothy L. Sayers*

God never promises us an easy journey in carpet slippers, but the way of a cross. *David Bentley*

The first thing about the cross is that it is a declaration of the way God is: not an attitude of 'Down on your knees you rotten little sinner' ... but a statement that God is vulnerable. *Michael Hare Duke*

If you are looking for an example of humility, look at the cross. *St Thomas Aquinas*

The cross is not a picture of God. This was God himself. *John Austin Baker*

That cross is a tree set on fire with invisible flame that illumineth all the world. That flame is love. *Thomas Traherne*

Crosses are ladders that lead to heaven. *English proverb*

The cross of Christ is the Jacob's ladder by which we ascend unto the highest heaven. *Thomas Traherne*

One who does not seek the cross of Jesus isn't seeking the glory of Christ. *St John of the Cross*

No cross, no crown. *English proverb*

No pain, no palm; no thorn, no throne. *William Penn*

It is the fellowship of the cross to experience the burden of the other. *Dietrich Bonhoeffer*

By the cross we know the gravity of sin and the greatness of God's love towards us. *St John Chrysostom*

Calvary is the key to an omnipotence which works only and always through sacrificial love. *Michael Ramsey*

It is true that he (Jesus) died of a broken body. It would be even truer to say, both medically and spiritually, that he died of a broken heart. *Eric S. Abbott*

The Lord's body became a bait for death, so that the dragon, hoping to swallow him up, would be forced to disgorge with him everyone else he had swallowed. *St Cyril of Jerusalem*

The figure of the Crucified invalidates all thought which takes success for its standard. *Dietrich Bonhoeffer*

The essential fact of Christianity is that God thought all men worth the sacrifice of his son. *William Barclay*

Easter

No resurrection. No Christianity. *Michael Ramsey*

Christianity is in its very essence a resurrection religion. The concept of resurrection lies at its heart. If you remove it, Christianity is destroyed. *John Stott*

The stone at the tomb of Jesus was a pebble to the Rock of Ages inside. *Frederick Beck*

There is no Easter without a Good Friday. *Matthew Fox*

If Christ be not risen, the dreadful consequence is not that death ends life, but that we are still in our sins. *G. A. Studdert-Kennedy*

Our Lord has written the promise of the resurrection, not in books alone, but in every leaf in springtime. *Martin Luther*

Easter is not part of the old accustomed divine order ... but it is an absolutely new, unexpected act of the living God. *Martin Niemoller*

At Easter let your clothes be new
Or else be sure you will it rue. *Traditional*

Ascension

The ascension of Christ is his liberation from all restrictions of time and space. It does not represent his removal from earth, but his constant presence everywhere on earth. *William Temple*

Pentecost

See 'Holy Spirit', p. 14

Harvest

We gather together in the chancel of our church on the first Sunday of next month and there receive, in the bread of our new corn, that blessed sacrament. *R. S. Hawker, announcing the first modern church celebration of harvest in September 1843*

At the Harvest Festival in church the area behind the pulpit was piled high with tins of fruit for the old-aged pensioners. We had collected the tinned fruit from door to door. Most of it came from old-aged pensioners. *Clive James in his* Unreliable Memoirs *(1980)*

Now God comes to thee ... as the sun at noon to illustrate all shadows, as the sheaves in harvest to fill all penuries, all occasions invite his mercies, and all times are his seasons. *John Donne in one of his* Sermons *(1625)*

Earth here is so kind, that just tickle her with a hoe and she laughs with a harvest. *Douglas Jerrold writing about Australia in his* Wit and Opinions

~ The Church and the Clergy ~

The Church

Mother Church. *Quintus Tertullian*

He cannot have God for his father who refuses to have the Church for his mother. *St Augustine of Hippo*

There is no salvation outside the Church. *St Cyprian*

No salvation exists outside the Church. *St Augustine of Hippo*

Every day people are straying away from the Church and going back to God. *Lenny Bruce*

The middle class in England did not wholly lose the habit of going to church until they acquired motor cars. *Charles Williams*

God pity the nation whose factory chimneys rise higher than her church spires. *John Kelman*

The Church of England is the perfect church for people who don't go to church. *Gerald Priestland*

The Christian Church is the one organization in the world that exists purely for the benefit of non-members. *William Temple*

The Church is the only institution in the world that has lower requirements than those for getting on a bus. *William Laroe*

Don't stay away from church because there are so many hypocrites. There's always room for one more. *Arthur R. Adams*

To be of no church is dangerous. Religion … will glide by degrees out of the mind. *Samuel Johnson*

The Lord showed me, so that I did see clearly, that he did not dwell in those temples which men had commanded and set up, but in people's hearts. *George Fox*

He who is near the church is often far from God. *French proverb*

To be a loyal churchman is hobbyism ... unless it is the way to be a loyal Christian. *Austin Farrer*

The Church ... is now largely associated with people's pastimes and leisure activities. People go to church in the same way they might play bowls or skittles or go to the pub. *Richard Harries*

Do not honour him [Christ] here in church by wearing silk, while you neglect him outside the church where he is cold and naked. *St John Chrysostom*

Help me, Lord, to remember that religion is not to be confined to the church ... nor exercised only in prayer and meditation, but that everywhere I am in thy presence. *Susanna Wesley*

Religion is a great force – the only real motive force in the world; but what you fellows don't understand is that you must get at a man through his own religion and not through yours. *George Bernard Shaw*

The church ... does not depend on excluding people and groups, but on a witness to the constantly inclusive activity of a God whose concern extends to a sparrow that falls on the ground. *Peter Selby*

I like the silent church before the service begins better than any preaching. *Ralph Waldo Emerson*

No sound ought to be heard in the Church but the healing voice of Christian charity. *Edmund Burke*

Our divisions prevent our neighbours from hearing the gospel as they should. *Pope John Paul II*

Sunday clears away the rust of the week. *Joseph Addison*

The Clergy

My parish is the gutter. *David Wilkerson*

I look upon the world as my parish. *John Wesley*

The priesthood is not about performing priestly functions. It is about *being* a priest, like being a father. *Graham Leonard*

The test of a vocation is the drudgery it involves. *Logan Pearsall Smith*

I always like to be associated with a lot of priests because it makes me understand anticlerical things so well. *Hilaire Belloc*

Avoid, as you would the plague, the clergyman who is also a man of business. *St Jerome*

A blot upon a layman's coat is little seen: a spot upon an alb cannot be hid. *Henry Manning*

Some clergy prepare their sermons; others prepare themselves. *Samuel Wilberforce*

Do not let your deeds belie your words, lest when you speak in church someone may say to himself, 'Why do you not practise what you preach?' *St Jerome*

The test of a preacher is that his congregation goes away saying, not 'What a lovely sermon!' but 'I will do something.' *St Francis de Sales*

He preaches well that lives well. *Cervantes*

The clergy should regard themselves as physicians of the soul. *William Ralph Inge*

Everything suffers by translation except a bishop. *Earl of Chesterfield*

Do pray for better bishops. *Edward King*

A bishop is most like God when he is silent. *St Ignatius Loyola*

A bishop should die preaching. *John Jewell*

Being a man I may come to be Pope. *Cervantes*

Anybody can be Pope; the proof of this is that I have become one. *Pope John XXIII in a letter to a boy wanting career advice*

~ Human Nature ~

Others

The habit of thinking ill of everything and everyone is tiresome to ourselves and to all around us. *Pope John XXIII*

I always prefer to believe the best of everybody; it saves so much trouble. *Rudyard Kipling*

It's not the world that's got so much worse but the news coverage that's got so much better. *G. K. Chesterton (attributed)*

The minority is sometimes right; the majority always wrong. *George Bernard Shaw*

Most of the trouble in the world is caused by people wanting to be important. *T. S. Eliot*

It is better to be faithful than famous. *Theodore Roosevelt*

Power corrupts, but lack of power corrupts absolutely. *Adlai Stevenson*

The best definition of man is the ungrateful biped. *Fyodor Dostoyevsky*

A cat can be trusted to purr when she is pleased, which is more than can be said about human beings. *William Ralph Inge*

Man is the only animal that laughs and weeps, for he is the only animal that is struck by the difference between what things are and what they might have been. *William Hazlitt*

Never trust a man who speaks well of everybody. *John Churton Collins*

Men always hate most what they envy most. *Henry L. Mencken*

Beware the fury of a patient man. *John Dryden*

When a man is wrapped up in himself, he makes a pretty small package. *John Ruskin*

It is a terrible fact that when men ignore God, they cease to be human. *E. C. Ratcliff*

Among those whom I like or admire, I can find no common denominator, but among those whom I love, I can: all of them make me laugh. *W. H. Auden*

Ourselves

We are all in the gutter, but some of us are looking at the stars. *Oscar Wilde*

It is human nature to think wisely and to act foolishly. *Anatole France*

It's often niceness that causes all the trouble. Niceness is a killer really. Niceness settles for mediocrity. *George Walden*

The urge to save humanity is almost always only a false-face for the urge to rule it. *Henry L. Mencken in 1956*

It is only people of small moral stature that have to stand on their dignity. *Arnold Bennett*

We can destroy ourselves by cynicism and disillusion, just as effectively as by bombs. *Kenneth Clark*

Except during the nine months before he draws his first breath, no man manages his affairs as well as a tree does. *George Bernard Shaw*

Character is what you are in the dark. *Dwight L. Moody*

No one ever became extremely wicked all at once. *Decimus Juvenal*

There is a great deal of unmapped country within us. *George Eliot*

We are all of us, more or less, the slaves of opinion. *William Hazlitt*

Man with all his noble qualities ... still bears in his bodily frame the indelible stamp of his lowly origin. *Charles Darwin*

The best may err. *Joseph Addison*

Most of us follow our conscience as we follow a wheelbarrow. We push it in front of us in the direction we want to go. *Billy Graham*

Our nature is very bad in itself, but very good to them that use it well. *Jeremy Taylor*

The man who never alters his opinion is like standing water, and breeds reptiles of the mind. *William Blake*

Man is the only animal that blushes. Or needs to. *Mark Twain*

Fine minds are seldom fine souls. *Johann Paul Richter*

People do not lack strength; they lack will. *Victor Hugo*

Our minds are lazier than our bodies. *La Rochefoucauld*

The great majority of men exist but do not live. *Benjamin Disraeli*

Almost all our thoughts are more pardonable than the methods we resort to to hide them. *La Rochefoucauld*

He who is in love with himself has at least this advantage – he won't encounter many rivals in his love. *Georg Christoph Lichtenberg*

We have just enough religion to make us hate, but not enough to make us love one another. *Jonathan Swift*

Perhaps there is only one cardinal sin: impatience. Because of impatience we were driven out of Paradise; because of impatience we cannot return. *Franz Kafka*

Must then a Christ perish in torment in every age to save those who have no imagination? *George Bernard Shaw in the epilogue to his play* St Joan

It is human to want things to be different. *Peter Selby*

Nothing astonishes men so much as common sense and plain dealing. *Ralph Waldo Emerson*

Nothing great was ever achieved without enthusiasm. *Ralph Waldo Emerson*

Encouragement is oxygen to the soul. *George M. Adams*

Self-Knowledge

'Know thyself?' If I knew myself, I'd run away. *Johann Goethe*

It often happens that I wake at night and begin to think about a serious problem and decide I must tell the Pope about it. Then I wake up completely and remember that I *am* the Pope. *Pope John XXIII*

I can live for two months on a good compliment. *Mark Twain*

How awful to reflect that what people say of us is true! *Logan Pearsall Smith*

The greatest of faults ... is to be conscious of none. *Thomas Carlyle*

The secret of being a bore is to tell everything. *Voltaire*

We are all capable of evil thoughts, but only very rarely of evil deeds: we can all do good deeds, but very few of us can think good thoughts. *Cesare Pavese*

The degree of one's emotion varies inversely with one's knowledge of the facts – the less you know, the hotter you get. *Bertrand Russell*

When angry, count ten before you speak; when very angry, count a hundred. *Thomas Jefferson*

However just your words, you spoil everything when you speak them with anger. *St John Chrysostom*

If we had no faults of our own, we would not take so much pleasure in noticing those of others. *La Rochefoucauld*

You will not become a saint through other people's sins. *Anton Chekhov*

The point of having an open mind, like having an open mouth, is to close it on something solid. *G. K. Chesterton*

A good person can put himself in the place of a bad person more easily than a bad person can put himself in the place of a good person. *Johann Paul Richter*

Moral indignation is jealousy with a halo. *H. G. Wells*

I will never be an old man. To me, old age is always fifteen years older than I am. *Bernard Baruch*

~ Baptism ~

Christians are made, not born. *St Jerome*

Being baptized, we are enlightened; being enlightened, we are adopted as children; being adopted, we are made perfect; being made complete, we are made immortal. *St Clement of Alexandria*

If anyone does not receive baptism, they have no salvation. *St Cyril of Jerusalem*

Know you what it is to be a child? ... It is to have a spirit yet [still] streaming from the waters of baptism; it is to believe in love, to believe in loveliness, to believe in belief. *Francis Thompson in the* Dublin Review *(1908)*

You are standing before God in the presence of the hosts of angels. The Holy Spirit is about to set his seal on each of your souls. You are about to be drawn into the service of the great king. *St Cyril of Jerusalem*

You were rubbed with oil like an athlete, Christ's athlete, as though in preparation for an earthly wrestling match. *St Ambrose*

When the Church baptizes a child, that action concerns me, for that child is thereby connected to ... that body of which I am a member. *John Donne*

Baptism seemed such an integral part of New Testament Christianity and I couldn't imagine a droplet of water dribbled on my head when I was a baby could be a proper substitute for that adult symbol of submission and obedience. *Cliff Richard*

Why did Christ refer to the grace of the Spirit under the name of water? Because through water all plants and animals live. *St Cyril of Jerusalem*

Happy is our sacrament of water, in that by washing away the sins of our early blindness, we are set free and admitted into eternal life. *Tertullian*

Baptism signifies that the old Adam in us is to be drowned by daily sorrow and repentance, and perish with all sins and evil lusts; and that the new man should daily come forth again and rise, who shall live before God in righteousness and purity forever. *Martin Luther*

The Passover provides the day of most solemnity for baptism, for then was accomplished our Lord's Passion, and into it we are baptized. *Quintus Tertullian*

His light is received by those who long for the splendour of perpetual light that can never be destroyed by darkness. *St Ambrose*

~ Love ~

The first duty of love is to listen. *Paul Tillich*

A soul cannot live without loving. It must have something to love, for it was created to love. *St Catherine of Siena*

The love of the soul is the sweetest thing in the world. *Thomas Traherne*

Take away love and our earth is a tomb. *Robert Browning*

For those who love, nothing is hard. *St Jerome*

Only love lasts for ever. Alone, it constructs the shape of eternity in the earthly and short-lived dimensions of the history of man on earth. *Pope John Paul II*

Joy is love exalted; peace is love in repose; long-suffering is love enduring; gentleness is love in society, goodness is love in action; faith is love on the battlefield; meekness is love in school; and temperance is love in training. *Dwight L. Moody*

Loving God

If thou knewest the whole Bible by heart, and the sayings of all the philosophers, what would it profit thee without the love of God? *Thomas à Kempis*

We should love God because he is God, and the measure of our love should be to love him without measure. *St Bernard of Clairvaux*

To love our neighbour in charity is to love God in man. *St Francis of Sales*

He who is filled with love is filled with God himself. *St Augustine of Hippo*

Only through love can we attain communion with God. *Albert Schweitzer*

Give me such love for God and men as will blot out all hatred and bitterness. *Dietrich Bonhoeffer*

Loving Others

Human beings must be known to be loved, but divine things must be loved to be known. *Blaise Pascal*

He alone loves the Creator perfectly who manifests a pure love for his neighbour. *Bede*

Love seeks one thing only: the good of the one loved. *Thomas Merton*

I was looking for someone to love, because I loved being a lover. *St Augustine of Hippo*

Where there is no love, pour love in, and you will draw love out. *St John of the Cross*

When you love someone, you love him as he is. *Charles Péguy*

Love is not to be purchased. *St Jerome*

The heart has its reasons which reason knows nothing of. *Blaise Pascal*

We are shaped and fashioned by what we love. *Johann Wolfgang von Goethe*

Next to the blessed sacrament itself, your neighbour is the holiest object presented to your senses. *C. S. Lewis*

Love is rarer than genius itself. And friendship is rarer than love. *Charles Péguy*

To see a young couple loving each other is no wonder; but to see an old couple loving each other is the best sight of all. *William Makepeace Thackeray*

In the evening of our lives, we shall be examined in love. *St John of the Cross*

Love your enemy – it'll drive him nuts. *Source unknown*

~ Friends and Neighbours ~

Being Alone

It is better to be alone than in bad company. *George Washington*

The greatest misfortune – to be incapable of solitude. *Jean de la Bruyère*

I have never found the companion that was so companionable as solitude. *Henry David Thoreau*

Language has created the word 'loneliness' to express the pain of being alone, and the word 'solitude' to express the glory of being alone. *Paul Tillich*

Settle yourself in solitude and you will come upon Him in yourself. *St Teresa of Avila*

People are lonely because they build walls instead of bridges. *Joseph F. Newton*

Pray that your loneliness may spur you into finding something to live for, great enough to die for. *Dag Hammarskjöld*

Individuals cannot cohere closely unless they sacrifice something of their individuality. *Robert H. Benson*

The fullness of the Christian life cannot be known except in fellowship – fellowship with God and fellowship with one another. *W. E. Sangster*

Hell is oneself. *T. S. Eliot*

Hell is other people. *Jean-Paul Sartre*

Friendship

A friend is long sought, hardly found, and with difficulty kept. *St Jerome*

Your friend is the man who knows all about you, and still likes you. *Elbert G. Hubbard writing in* The Notebook (*1927*)

A true friend is the most precious of all possessions and the one we take least thought about acquiring. *La Rochefoucauld*

A friend is a person with whom I may be sincere. Before him, I may think aloud. *Ralph Waldo Emerson*

In friendship nobody has a double. *Friedrich von Schiller*

Friendship is in loving rather than in being loved. *Robert Bridges*

Nature teaches us to love our friends but religion our enemies. *Thomas Fuller*

We can live without our friends but not without our neighbours. *Thomas Fuller*

You make more friends by becoming interested in other people than by trying to interest other people in yourself. *Dale Carnegie*

Everybody's friend is nobody's. *Arthur Schopenhauer*

Who boasts to have won a multitude of friends has ne'er had one. *Samuel Taylor Coleridge*

Most people enjoy the inferiority of their best friends. *Earl of Chesterfield*

The friendship that can cease has never been real. *St Jerome*

Sometimes we owe a friend to the lucky circumstance that we give him no cause for envy. *Friedrich Wilhelm Nietzsche*

The more we love our friends, the less we flatter them. *Molière*

It is mutual respect which makes friendship lasting. *John Henry Newman*

True friendship ought never to conceal what it thinks. *St Jerome*

A friend in power is a friend lost. *Henry Adams*

God evidently does not intend us all to be rich or powerful or great, but he does intend us all to be friends. *Ralph Waldo Emerson*

Shared joys make a friend, not shared sufferings. *Friedrich Wilhelm Nietzsche*

Friendships begun in this world will be taken up again, never to be broken off. *St Francis de Sales*

The language of friendship is not words but meanings. *Henry David Thoreau*

Neighbours

He alone loves the Creator perfectly who manifests a pure love for his neighbour. *Bede*

I say that Christ ... might be living now in the world as our next-door neighbour and perhaps we not find it out. *John Henry Newman*

How rarely we weigh our neighbour in the same balance in which we weigh ourselves. *Thomas à Kempis*

Love your neighbour, yet pull not down your hedge. *George Herbert*

You can never love your neighbour without loving God. *Jacques Bénigne Bossuet*

Relationships

We are born helpless. As soon as we are fully conscious we discover loneliness. We need others physically, emotionally, intellectually; we need them if we are to know anything, even ourselves. *C. S. Lewis*

Keep company with the more cheerful sort of the godly; there is no mirth like the mirth of believers. *Richard Baxter*

He that converses not, knows nothing. *Thomas Fuller*

Two may talk and one may hear, but three cannot take part in a conversation of the most sincere and searching part. *Ralph Waldo Emerson*

One can bear grief, but it takes two to be glad. *Elbert G. Hubbard*

The more a man knows, the more he forgives. *Catherine the Great*

Could we read the the secret history of our enemies, we should find in each man's life, sorrow and suffering enough to disarm all hostility. *Henry Wadsworth Longfellow*

If you want a person's faults, go to those who love him. They will not tell you but they know. *Robert Louis Stevenson*

If we say that we do a thing for Christ's sake or for God's sake it may sound and it can mean that we do it not for the sake of the needy. It is like the woman giving a tramp some bread. 'Not for your sake, my man,' she said, 'but for God's sake.' To which the tramp replied, 'Then for Christ's sake put some butter on it.' *Howard Williams in* Down to Earth

To put man and woman upon equality is not to elevate woman but to degrade her. *Henry Manning*

Being a woman is a terribly difficult trade, since it consists principally of dealing with men. *Joseph Conrad*

The history of women is the history of the worst form of tyranny the world has ever known. *Oscar Wilde*

~ The Common Good ~

There is no higher religion than human service. To work for the common good is the greatest creed. *Albert Schweitzer*

Have thy tools ready; God will find thee work. *Charles Kingsley*

Do what you can, with what you have, where you are. *Theodore Roosevelt*

Employ whatever God has entrusted you with, in doing good, all possible good, in every possible kind and degree. *John Wesley*

Nobody makes a greater mistake than he who does nothing because he could only do a little. *Edmund Burke*

Great works do not always lie in our way, but every moment we may do little ones excellently. *St Francis de Sales*

Every day the choice between good and evil is presented to us in simple ways. *W. E. Sangster*

There is a limit at which forbearance ceases to be a virtue. *Edmund Burke*

Extremism in the defence of liberty is no vice. And moderation in the pursuit of justice is no virtue. *Barrie Goldwater*

I find life an exciting business, and most exciting when it is lived for others. *Helen Keller*

It is by those who have suffered that the world has been advanced. *Leo Tolstoy*

First they came for the Jews. I was silent. I was not a Jew. Then they came for the Communists. I was silent. I was not a Communist. Then they came for the trade unionists. I was silent. I was not a trade unionist. Then they came for me. There was no one left to speak for me. *Martin Niemoller*

The only thing necessary for the triumph of evil is for good men to do nothing. *Edmund Burke*

Man must know that in this theatre of man's life it is reserved only for God and angels to be lookers on. *Francis Bacon*

I can't talk religion to a man with bodily hunger in his eyes. *George Bernard Shaw*

You must live with people to know their problems, and live with God in order to solve them. *P. T. Forsyth*

Human blood is all of one colour. *Thomas Fuller*

Charity is the pure gold which makes us rich in eternal wealth. *Jean Pierre Camus*

For a war to be just, three conditions are necessary – public authority, just cause, right motive. *St Thomas Aquinas*

Older men declare war. But it is youth that must fight and die. *Herbert Hoover*

As long as war is regarded as wicked, it will always have its fascination. When it is looked upon as vulgar, it will cease to be popular. *Oscar Wilde*

Sometime they'll give a war and nobody will come. *Carl Sandburg*

We must have military power to keep madmen from taking over the world. *Billy Graham*

For a Christian who believes in Jesus and his gospel, war is an iniquity and a contradiction. *Pope John XXIII*

To be prepared for war is one of the most effectual ways of preserving peace. *George Washington*

The Church knows nothing of the sacredness of war. The Church that prays 'Our Father' asks God only for peace. *Dietrich Bonhoeffer*

Christians by definition are a possible danger to any state. *Colin Morris*

We can't enrich the common good of our country by driving out those we don't care for. *Oscar Romero*

Wickedness is always easier than virtue for it takes the short cut to everything. *Samuel Johnson*

If I were asked to state the great objective which Church and State are both demanding for the sake of every man and woman and child in this country, I would say that great objective is 'a more abundant life'. *Franklin D. Roosevelt*

It may be that the day of judgement will dawn tomorrow; in that case we shall gladly stop working for a better future. But not before. *Dietrich Bonhoeffer*

Men never do evil so completely and cheerfully as when they do it from religious conviction. *Blaise Pascal*

God is the judge of all social systems. *Oscar Romero*

~ Weddings ~

Marriage is a great institution – no family should be without it. *Bob Hope*

Advice to persons about to marry: Don't. *Punch, 1845*

Marriage is like life in this – that it is a field of battle, and not a bed of roses. *Robert Louis Stevenson*

When two people are under the influence of the most violent, most insane, most delusive and most transient of passions, they are required to swear that they will remain in that excited, abnormal and exhausting condition continuously until death do them part. *George Bernard Shaw*

The music at a wedding procession always reminds me of the music of soldiers going into battle. *Heinrich Heine*

Marriage resembles a pair of shears, so joined that they cannot be separated, often moving in opposite directions yet always punishing anyone who comes between them. *P. Fontaine*

Marriage has many pains, but celibacy has no pleasures. *Samuel Johnson*

True love is like seeing ghosts; we all talk about it, but few of us have ever seen one. *La Rochefoucauld*

Love does not consist in gazing at each other but in looking together in the same direction. *Antoine de Saint-Exupéry*

Love does not dominate; it cultivates. *Johann Goethe*

Habit is everything – even in love. *Marquis de Vauvenargues*

A successful marriage is an edifice that needs to be rebuilt every day. *André Maurois*

It is as absurd to say that a man can't love one woman all the time as it is to say that a violinist needs several violins to play the same piece of music. *Honoré de Balzac*

There are two kinds of faithfulness in love: one is based on forever finding new things to love in the loved one; the other is based on our pride in being faithful. *La Rochefoucauld*

No disguise can long conceal love where it exists, or long feign it where it is lacking. *La Rochefoucauld*

Sexuality throws no light upon love, but only through love can we learn to understand sexuality. *Eugen Rosenstock-Huessy*

~ Family Life ~

Where does the family start? It starts with a young man falling in love with a girl – no superior alternative has yet been found. *Winston Churchill (attributed)*

You will never be nearer to Christ than in caring for the one man, the one woman, the one child. *Michael Ramsey*

It is easier for a father to have children than for children to have a real father. *Pope John XXIII*

The most important thing a father can do for his children is to love their mother. *Theodore M. Hesburgh*

I think it must somewhere be written that the virtues of the mothers shall be visited on their children as well as the sins of their fathers. *Charles Dickens*

Mother is the name of God in the lips and hearts of little children. *William Makepeace Thackeray*

No man is poor who has had a godly mother. *Abraham Lincoln*

There is no limit to the power of a good woman. *Robert H. Benson*

Women should remain at home, sit still, keep house, and bear and bring up children. *Martin Luther*

Babies do not want to hear about babies; they like to be told of giants and castles. *Samuel Johnson*

The real menace in dealing with a five-year-old is that in no time at all you begin to sound like a five-year-old. *Jean Kerr*

You can learn many things from children. How much patience you have, for instance. *Franklin P. Jones*

If a child tells a lie, tell him he has told a lie, but don't call him a liar. If you define him as a liar, you break down his confidence in his own character. *Johann Paul Richter*

Unlike grown-ups, children have little need to deceive themselves. *Johann Goethe*

Parentage is a very important profession; but no test of fitness for it is ever imposed in the interest of the children. *George Bernard Shaw*

The joys of parents are secret; and so are their griefs and fears. *Francis Bacon*

Children begin by loving their parents. After a while they judge them. Rarely, if ever, do they forgive them. *Oscar Wilde*

We never know the love of the parent until we become parents ourselves. *Henry Ward Beecher*

A child tells in the street what its father and mother say at home. *The Jewish Talmud*

Every word and deed of a parent is a fibre woven into the character of a child. *David Wilkerson*

There is just one way to bring up a child in the way that he should go and that is to travel that way yourself. *Abraham Lincoln*

I have found out the best way to give advice to your children is to find out what they want and then advise them to do it. *Harry S. Truman in a 1955 television interview*

A family is a unit composed not only of children, but of men, women, an occasional animal, and the common cold. *Ogden Nash*

Home life as we understand it is no more natural to us than a cage is to a cockatoo. *George Bernard Shaw in the preface to his play* Getting Married

It is an evident truth, that most of the mischiefs that now infest or seize upon mankind ... are caused by the disorders or ill-governedness of families. *Richard Baxter*

Every effort to make society sensitive to the importance of the family is a great service to humanity. *Pope John Paul II*

All happy families resemble one another; every unhappy family is unhappy in its own way. *Leo Tolstoy*

A family that prays together stays together. *Mother Teresa*

A home is no home unless it contains food and fire for the mind as well as for the body. *Margaret Fuller*

The union of the family lies in love. *Robert H. Benson*

Home is where the heart is. *Pliny the Elder*

The work that all can do is to make a small home circle brighter and better. *George Eliot*

Happy is the house that shelters a friend. *Ralph Waldo Emerson*

~ Our Daily Bread ~

Food and Drink

The history of man from the beginning has been the history of the struggle for daily bread. *Jesus de Castro*

There's no sauce in the world like hunger. *Cervantes*

Remember that there must be someone to cook the meals, and count yourselves happy in being able to serve like Martha. *St Teresa of Avila*

Strange to see how a good dinner and feasting reconciles everybody. *Samuel Pepys*

Thank God for tea! What would the world do without tea? – How did it exist? I am glad I was not born before tea. *Sydney Smith*

It was a common saying among the Puritans, 'Brown bread and the gospel is good fare.' *Matthew Henry*

There is no such thing as 'my' bread. All bread is *ours* and is given to me, to others through me and to me through others. *Meister Eckhart*

Christians should offer their brethren simple and unpretentious hospitality. *St Basil*

It takes more oil than vinegar to make a good salad. *Jean Pierre Camus*

Thanks be to God, since my leaving drinking of wine, I do find myself much better, and do mind my business better, and do spend less money, and less time lost in idle company. *Samuel Pepys*

To fast is to learn to love and appreciate food, and one's own good fortune in having it. *Monica Furlong*

Do not limit the benefits of fasting merely to abstinence from food, for a true fast means refraining from evil. *St Ambrose*

Abstinence is as easy to me, as temperance would be difficult. *Samuel Johnson*

When the stomach is full it is easy to talk of fasting. *St Jerome*

Eat to live, and do not live to eat. *Benjamin Franklin*

Food ought to be a refreshment for the body and not a burden. *St Bonaventure*

Eat not to dullness, drink not to elevation. *Benjamin Franklin*

One ought to rise from a meal able to apply oneself to prayer and study. *St Jerome*

I'm only a beer teetotaller, not a champagne teetotaller. *George Bernard Shaw in his play* Candida

Bless me Lord, and let my food strengthen me to serve thee. *Isaac Watts*

The test of our progress is not whether we add more to the abundance of those who have much; it is whether we provide enough for those who have too little. *Franklin D. Roosevelt*

We take excellent care of our bodies, which we have only for a lifetime, yet we let our souls shrivel, which we will have for eternity. *Billy Graham*

Money and Possessions

Money is like muck, no good except it be spread. *Francis Bacon*

The world is meant to be like a household in which all the servants receive equal allowances, for all men are equal. *St John Chrysostom*

If you make money your god, it will plague you like the devil. *Henry Fielding*

Chains of gold are no less chains than chains of iron. *François Fénelon*

Riches are gotten with pain, kept with care and lost with grief. *Thomas Fuller*

Riches are the beginning of all vices, because they make us capable of carrying out even our most vicious desires. *St Ambrose*

Riches are a good handmaid, but the worst mistress. *Francis Bacon*

Riches have made more covetous men than covetousness hath made rich men. *Thomas Fuller*

It is better to live rich than to die rich. *Samuel Johnson*

Nothing that is God's is obtainable by money. *Quintus Tertullian*

The real measure of our wealth is how much we'd be worth if we lost all our money. *John Henry Jowett*

The wealthy consume a great deal more than can be justified by the population figures. *Desmond Tutu*

If a person gets his attitude toward money straight, it will help straighten out almost every other area in his life. *Billy Graham*

Make all you can, save all you can, give all you can. *John Wesley*

He who has money to spare has it always in his power to benefit others: and of such power a good man must always be desirous. *Samuel Johnson*

For every one hundred men who can stand adversity there is only one who can withstand prosperity. *Thomas Carlyle*

Great wealth and content seldom live together. *Thomas Fuller*

Unless he has genius, a rich man cannot imagine what poverty is like. *Charles Péguy*

The golden age only comes to men when they have forgotten gold. *G. K. Chesterton*

God has given us two hands – one for receiving and the other for giving. *Billy Graham*

God gives when he will, as he will and to whom he will. *St Teresa of Avila*

It is right to be contented with what we have but never with what we are. *James Mackintosh*

Theirs is an endless road, a hopeless maze, who seek for goods before they seek for God. *St Bernard of Clairvaux*

In my experience the men who want something for nothing are invariably Christians. *George Bernard Shaw*

~ For Teachers and Students ~

For every person wishing to teach, there are thirty not wanting to be taught. *Source unknown*

School days, I believe, are the unhappiest in the whole span of human existence. They are full of dull, unintelligibly tasks, new and unpleasant ordinances, brutal violations of common sense and common decency. *H. L. Mencken writing in the* Baltimore Evening Sun *in 1928*

You teach your daughters the diameters of the planets, and wonder when you have done that they do not delight in your company. *Samuel Johnson*

The secret of education lies in respecting the pupil. *Ralph Waldo Emerson*

Education is what you give to children; training is what you do to plants. *Stephen Fry (speaking on BBC Radio 4)*

The whole point of education is that it should give a man abstract and eternal standards. *G. K. Chesterton*

Anyone who stops learning is old, whether at twenty or eighty. Anyone who keeps learning stays young. *Henry Ford*

People need to be reminded more often than they need to be instructed. *Samuel Johnson*

Children must be taught some sort of religion. Secular religion is an impossibility. Secular education comes to this: that the only reason for ceasing to do evil and learning to do well is that if you do not you will be caned. *George Bernard Shaw in the Preface to his play* Misalliance

Children are our most valuable natural resource. *Herbert Hoover*

Give me a child for the first seven years, and you may do what you like with him afterwards. *Francis Xavier*

The aim of education is the knowledge not of fact but of values. *William Ralph Inge in* The Church in the World *(1932)*

The supreme end of education is ... the power to tell the good from the bad, the genuine from the counterfeit, and to prefer the good and the genuine to the bad and the counterfeit. *Samuel Johnson*

The highest education is that which brings the student face to face, not simply with something great but with someone great, namely Christ. *Donald Coggan*

It is well to remember from time to time that nothing that is worth knowing can be taught. *Oscar Wilde in* The Critic As Artist *(1890)*

He who can, does. He who cannot, teaches. *George Bernard Shaw in his* Maxims for Revolutionists *(1903)*

There is but one thing in the world really worth pursuing – the knowledge of God. *Robert H. Benson*

I consider that the one who knows how to form the mind of the young is truly greater than all painters, sculptors and others like that. *St John Chrysostom*

What greater work is there than training the mind and forming the habits of the young? *St John Chrysostom*

A teacher affects eternity; he can never tell where his influence stops. *Henry Brooks Adams*

Headmasters have powers at their disposal with which Prime Ministers have never yet been invested. *Winston Churchill in* My Early Life

Lessons are not given, they are taken. *Cesare Pavese*

The gift of teaching is a peculiar talent, and implies a need and a craving in the teacher himself. *John Jay Chapman*

Example is always more efficacious than precept. *Samuel Johnson*

Example is not the main thing in influencing others – it is the only thing. *Albert Schweitzer*

Books are not absolutely dead things, but do contain a potency of life in them to be as active as that soul was whose progeny they are. *John Milton*

A good book is the precious lifeblood of a master spirit. *John Milton*

Those who know the least obey the best. *George Farquhar*

They know enough who know how to learn. *Henry Brooks Adams*

~ Experience ~

When I grow up, I want to be a little boy. *Joseph Heller in his novel* Something Happened

Youth would be an ideal state if it came a little later in life. *Lord Asquith speaking in 1923*

Youth is a wonderful thing; what a shame to waste it on children. *George Bernard Shaw*

A man that is young in years may be old in hours. *Francis Bacon*

Experience: the name everyone gives to their mistakes. *Oscar Wilde*

Experience is not what happens to a man. It is what a man does with what happens to him. *Aldous Huxley*

It is a good thing to follow the First Law of Holes; if you are in one, stop digging. *Denis Healey*

To reach something good it is very useful to have gone astray, and thus acquire experience. *St Teresa of Avila*

All experience is an arch to build upon. *Henry Brooks Adams*

Experience is the best of schoolmasters, only the school fees are heavy. *Thomas Carlyle*

There is no education like adversity. *Benjamin Disraeli*

Never be ashamed to own you have been in the wrong, 'tis but saying you are wiser today than you were yesterday. *Jonathan Swift*

To most men, experience is like the stern lights of a ship, which illumine only the track it has passed. *Samuel Taylor Coleridge*

Critics are people who know the way but can't drive the car. *Kenneth Tynan*

Too bad all the people who know how to run the country are busy driving taxi cabs and cutting hair. *George Burns*

The fact that an opinion has been widely held is no evidence whatever that it is not utterly absurd. *Bertrand Russell*

If nobody ever said anything unless he knew what he was talking about, a ghastly hush would descend upon earth. *Sir Alan Herbert*

Wisdom consists in knowing when and how to speak and when and where to keep silent. *Jean Pierre Camus*

Fools rush in where angels fear to tread. *Alexander Pope*

The greatest lesson in life is to know that even fools are right sometimes. *Winston Churchill*

Suffer fools gladly. They may be right. *Holbrook Jackson*

Embarrassment is the one ailment that lessens with age. *Craig Brown*

Everything has been said already, but since no one listens, one must always start again. *André Gide*

Life is learning to love. *Cicely Saunders*

Life is like playing a violin solo in public and learning the instrument as one goes on. *Samuel Butler*

Adventure is the champagne of life. *G. K. Chesterton*

Arouse yourself, gird your loins, put aside idleness, grasp the nettle and do some hard work. *St Bernard of Clairvaux*

A wise man will make more opportunities than he finds. *Francis Bacon*

No one is suddenly made perfect. *The Venerable Bede*

People seldom improve when they have no other model but themselves to copy after. *Oliver Goldsmith*

Man lives a really human life thanks to culture. *Pope John Paul II*

Worry does not empty tomorrow of its sorrow; it empties today of its strength. *Corrie ten Boom*

The safest road to hell is the gradual one – the gentle slope, soft underfoot, without sudden turnings, without milestones, without signposts. *C. S. Lewis*

I am always content with what happens; for I know that what God chooses is better than what I choose. *Epictetus*

To grow old is to pass from passion to compassion. *Albert Camus*

The old believe everything: the middle-aged suspect everything: the young know everything. *Oscar Wilde*

Old people like to give good advice, as solace for no longer being able to provide bad examples. *La Rochefoucauld*

You know you're getting old when the candles cost more than the cake. *Bob Hope*

No wise man ever wished to be younger. *Jonathan Swift*

One of the many pleasures of old age is giving things up. *Malcolm Muggeridge*

The greatest problem about old age is the fear that it may go on too long. *A. J. P. Taylor*

Few people know how to be old. *La Rochefoucauld*

Nothing is more beautiful than cheerfulness in an old face. *Johann Paul Richter*

In seed time, learn, in harvest teach, in winter enjoy. *William Blake*

~ The Good Life ~

Pleasure

Pleasure is something that you feel that you should really enjoy ... but you don't; and sin's something that you're quite sure you shouldn't enjoy but do. *Ralph Wightman*

A lifetime of happiness! No man alive could bear it: it would be hell on earth. *George Bernard Shaw*

You will always have joy in the evening if you spend the day fruitfully. *Thomas à Kempis*

Too many Christians envy the sinners their pleasure and the saints their joy, because they don't have either one. *Martin Luther*

You have to be serious, but never be solemn, because if you are solemn about anything there is the risk of becoming solemn about yourself. *Michael Ramsey*

Those who bring sunshine to the lives of others cannot keep it from themselves. *J. M. Barrie*

God cannot give us happiness and peace apart from himself, because it is not there. *C. S. Lewis*

Happy people have no history. *Fyodor Dostoyevsky*

The way to be happy is not to mind about happiness, just to set your heart on being true. And happiness will follow. *Wendy Beckett*

All of man's unhappiness stems from his inability to stay in a room alone. *Blaise Pascal*

We should have much peace if we would not busy ourselves with the sayings and doings of others. *Thomas à Kempis*

The soul is the wife of the body. They do not have the same kind of pleasure or, at least, they seldom enjoy it at the same time. *Paul Valéry*

If we only wanted to be happy, it would be easy; but we want to be happier than other people, which is almost always difficult, since we think them happier than they are. *Baron de Montesquieu*

It's pretty hard to tell what does bring happiness; poverty and wealth have both failed. *Kin Hubbard*

Nothing is more hopeless than a scheme of merriment. *Samuel Johnson*

If only we'd stop trying to be happy we could have a pretty good time. *Edith Wharton*

None are so old as those who have outlived enthusiasm. *Henry David Thoreau*

He who laughs, lasts. *Mary Pettibone Poole*

Morality

Grub first, then ethics. *Bertolt Brecht*

Love and *then* what you will, do. *St Augustine of Hippo*

One must never confuse error and the person who errs. *Pope John XXIII*

It is better that ten guilty persons escape than one innocent suffer. *William Blackstone*

Right is right, even if everyone is against it; and wrong is wrong, even if everyone is for it. *William Penn*

No man can break any of the Ten Commandments. He can only break himself against them. *G. K. Chesterton*

There is something wrong with a man if he does not want to break the Ten Commandments. *G. K. Chesterton*

Standards are always out of date. That is what makes them standards. *Alan Bennett in his play* Forty Years On

The devil is a gentleman who never goes where he is not welcome. *John L. Lincoln*

It is tempting to deny the existence of evil since denying it obviates the need to fight it. *Alexis Carrel*

You can never love your neighbour without loving God. *Jacques Bénigne Bossuet*

Using One's Talents

Talent is the capacity of doing anything that depends on application and industry. *William Hazlitt*

A milkmaid can milk cows to the glory of God. *Martin Luther*

A man can do only what he can do. But if he does that each day he can sleep at night and do it again the next day. *Albert Schweitzer*

Alas for those who never sing, but die with all their music in them. *Oliver Wendell Holmes*

I like work, it fascinates me. I can sit and look at it for hours. *Jerome K. Jerome*

You can do very little with faith, but you can nothing without it. *Nicholas M. Butler*

Without the support of faith, good works cannot stand. *St Ambrose*

God helps those who help themselves. *Benjamin Franklin (perhaps based on the saying of Aesop: The gods help those who help themselves)*

~ In Sickness and in Health ~

Sickness

He cures most in whom most have faith. *Galen*

The prayer that reforms the sinner and heals the sick is an absolute faith that all things are possible to God. *Mary Baker Eddy*

In sorrow and suffering, go straight to God with confidence, and you will be strengthened, enlightened and instructed. *St John of the Cross*

In moods of discouragement or despair, never forget that the sunshine will ultimately come back, that its absence never is permanent. Hang onto your faith, knowing that soon you will rise into the sunshine again. *Norman Vincent Peale*

If you bear your cross cheerfully, it will bear you. *Thomas à Kempis*

It is always darkest just before the day dawneth. *Thomas Fuller*

'Tis healthy to be sick sometimes. *Henry David Thoreau*

Stay till I am well, and *then* you shall tell me how to cure myself. *Samuel Johnson*

Pain is no evil unless it conquer us. *Charles Kingsley*

To live is to suffer; to survive is to find meaning in suffering. *Viktor Frankl*

Suffer with Christ, and for Christ, if you desire to reign with Christ. *Thomas à Kempis*

Our suffering is not worthy the name of suffering. When I consider my crosses, tribulations, and temptations, I shame myself almost to death, thinking what are they in comparison of the sufferings of my blessed Saviour Christ Jesus. *Martin Luther*

A Christian is someone who shares the sufferings of God in the world. *Dietrich Bonhoeffer*

Is life so wretched? Isn't it rather your hands which are too small, your vision which is muddied? You are the one who must grow up. *Dag Hammarskjöld*

What seem to us as bitter trials are often blessings in disguise. *Oscar Wilde*

Although the world is full of suffering, it is also full of the overcoming of it. *Helen Keller*

Make sickness itself a prayer. *St Francis de Sales*

How melancholy it is that we must often bolster up our will to live and strive by the thought that someone else is in an even worse plight than we are ourselves. *Oscar Wilde*

I have pain (there is no arguing against sense) but I have peace. I have peace. *Richard Baxter*

Caring and Curing

Before all things and above all things, care must be taken of the sick, so that they may be served in every deed as Christ himself. *St Benedict*

Care more for the individual patient than for the special features of the disease. *William Osler*

The best doctors in the world are Doctor Diet, Doctor Quiet and Doctor Merryman. *Jonathan Swift*

Medicine is the only profession that labours incessantly to destroy the reason for its existence. *James Bryce*

Stronger than all the evils in the soul is the Word, and the healing power that dwells in him. *Origen*

The all-sufficient Physician of humanity, the Saviour, heals both our body and our soul. *St Clement of Alexandria*

Health

Exercise is bunk. If you are healthy, you don't need it: if you are sick, you shouldn't take it. *Attributed to Henry Ford*

Health and cheerfulness mutually beget each other. *Joseph Addison*

Myself in constant good health, and in a most handsome and thriving condition. Blessed be Almighty God for it. *Samuel Pepys*

Take care of your health that it may serve you to serve God. *St Francis de Sales*

Be careful to preserve your health. It is a trick of the devil, which he employs to deceive good souls, to incite them to do more than they are able, in order that they may no longer be able to do anything. *St Vincent de Paul*

God whispers in our pleasures but shouts in our pain. *C. S. Lewis*

The whole point of this life is the healing of the heart's eye through which God is seen. *St Augustine of Hippo*

~ Hope ~

The utmost we can hope for in this life is contentment. *Joseph Addison*

Hope is itself a species of happiness, and perhaps, the chief happiness which the world affords. *Samuel Johnson*

Hope is the power of being cheerful in circumstances which we know to be desperate. *G. K. Chesterton*

Hope is a good breakfast, but it is a bad supper. *Francis Bacon in his* Apothegems *(1626)*

An idealist is one who, on noticing that a rose smells better than a cabbage, concludes that it will also make better soup. *H. L. Mencken*

It is impossible for that man to despair who remembers that his helper is omnipotent. *Jeremy Taylor*

Some men can live up to their loftiest ideals without ever going higher than a basement. *Theodore Roosevelt*

We promise according to our hopes and perform according to our fears. *La Rochefoucauld*

A religious hope does not only bear up the mind under her sufferings, but makes her rejoice in them. *Joseph Addison*

It is more serious to lose hope than to sin. *John of Carpathos*

It is only when everything is hopeless that hope begins to be a strength at all. *G. K. Chesterton*

The weakest of sinners can either frustrate or crown a hope of God. *Charles Péguy*

Whatever enlarges hope will also exalt courage. *Samuel Johnson*

Women, we need you to give us back our faith in humanity. *Desmond Tutu*

Patience and diligence, like faith, remove mountains. *William Penn*

He said not, 'Thou shalt not be tempested, thou shalt not be travailed, thou shalt not be afflicted;' but he said, 'Thou shalt not be overcome.' *Julian of Norwich*

Weak things united become strong. *Thomas Fuller*

An idea that is not dangerous is unworthy of being called an idea at all. *Oscar Wilde*

He who has health has hope and he who has hope has everything. *Arab proverb, source unknown*

Great hope makes great men. *Thomas Fuller*

If you do not hope, you will not find out what is beyond your hopes. *St Clement of Alexandria*

The word which God has written on the brow of every man is hope. *Victor Hugo*

~ Praise and Thanksgiving ~

Praise

Wonder is the basis of worship. *Thomas Carlyle*

The happiest man is he who learns from nature the lesson of worship. *Ralph Waldo Emerson*

Happiness is neither within us only, or without us; it is the union of ourselves with God. *Blaise Pascal*

Happiness is a mystery like religion, and should never be rationalised. *G. K. Chesterton*

Happiness is the natural life of man. *St Thomas Aquinas*

When I think upon my God, my heart is so full of joy that the notes dance and leap from my pen. *Franz Josef Haydn*

We are all strings in the concert of his joy. *Jacob Boehme*

Joy is the serious business of heaven. *C. S. Lewis*

To rejoice at another person's joy is like being in heaven. *Meister Eckhart*

Do not forget that even as 'to work is to worship', so to be cheery is to worship also. *Robert Louis Stevenson*

It is only when men begin to worship that they begin to grow. *Calvin Coolidge*

A little lifting of the heart suffices. *Brother Lawrence*

It is a man's duty to praise and bless God and pay him due thanks. *Epictetus*

Worship, then, is not a part of the Christian life; it is the Christian life. *Gerald Vann*

Thanksgiving

Happiness is the sublime moment when you get out of your corsets at night. *Joyce Grenfell (attributed)*

We should spend as much time in thanking God for his benefits as we do in asking him for them. *St Vincent de Paul*

God waits for the chances we give him to show his great generosity. *St John Chrysostom*

One act of thanksgiving when things go wrong with us is worth a thousand thanks when things are agreeable to our inclination. *St John of Avila*

Thank God every morning when you get up that you have something to do which must be done whether you like it or not. *Charles Kingsley*

Blessed is he who expects no gratitude for he shall not be disappointed. *W. C. Bennett*

No duty is more urgent than that of returning thanks. *St Ambrose*

Let gratitude for the past inspire us with trust for the future. *François Fénelon*

My Lord, I thank you for having created me. *St Clare of Assisi*

Accept the fact that you are accepted. *Paul Tillich*

Thanksgiving is the end of all human conduct, whether observed in words or works. *Joseph Barber Lightfoot*

For what has been – thanks! For what shall be – yes! *Dag Hammarskjöld*

Gratitude is not only the greatest of virtues but the parent of all others. *Marcus Tullius Cicero*

It is only with gratitude that life becomes rich. *Dietrich Bonhoeffer*

Gratitude is heaven itself. *William Blake*

Thou who hast given so much to me, give me one more thing –
a grateful heart! *George Herbert*

Too much of a good thing is wonderful. *Mae West*

~ Repentance ~

'Oh God, if I was sure I were to die tonight I would repent at once.' It is the commonest prayer in all languages. *J. M. Barrie*

Give me chastity and continency but do not give it yet. *St Augustine in his* Confessions *(397–401)*

We don't call it sin today, we call it self-expression. *Mary Stocks*

I can resist everything except temptation. *Oscar Wilde in his play* Lady Windermere's Fan

That which we call sin in others is experiment for us. *Ralph Waldo Emerson*

It is human to err; it is devilish to remain wilfully in error. *St Augustine of Hippo*

Sleep with clean hands, either kept clean all day by integrity or washed clean at night by repentance. *John Donne*

There is only one thing to be feared, and that is sin. Everything else is beside the point. *St John Chrysostom*

Men are not punished for their sins, but by them. *Elbert G. Hubbard*

It may well be that human sins afflict with grief even God himself. *Origen*

All saints have a past and all sinners have a future. *Anton Chekhov*

No man need stay the way he is. *Harry Emerson Fosdick*

The power of choosing between good and evil is within us all. *Origen*

Sin is always a squandering of our humanity, a squandering of one of our most precious values. *Pope John Paul II*

There is no faith without repentance. *Martin Niemoller*

Confession: the acknowledgement made to a priest of a sinful act committed by a friend, neighbour or acquaintance and to which you reacted with righteous indignation. *Ambrose Bierce in* The Devil's Dictionary, *1911*

I turn over a new leaf every day – but the blots show through. *Keith Waterhouse in his novel* Billy Liar

O Lord, forgive what I have been, sanctify what I am, and order what I shall be. *Thomas Wilson*

It used to irritate a friend of mine that when he went to confession he never got the chance to tell the priest the good things he had done. *Monica Furlong*

Being entirely honest with oneself is a good exercise. *Sigmund Freud*

The knowledge of sin is the beginning of salvation. *Epicurus*

The confession of evil works is the first beginning of good works. *St Augustine of Hippo*

Love truth but pardon error. *Voltaire*

If we only have the will to walk, then God is pleased with our stumbles. *C. S. Lewis*

Where there is yet shame, there may be time for virtue. *Samuel Johnson*

No man is so perfect and holy as not to have sometimes temptations. *Thomas à Kempis*

The Lord is loving unto a man, and swift to pardon, but slow to punish. Let no man therefore despair of his own salvation. *St Cyril of Jerusalem*

I think that if God forgives us we must forgive ourselves. *C. S. Lewis*

No one is redeemed except through unmerited mercy, and no one is condemned except through merited judgement. *St Augustine of Hippo*

It is by forgiving that one is forgiven. *Mother Teresa*

To err is human, to forgive divine. *Alexander Pope*

To sin is human, but to persist in sin is devilish. *St Catherine of Siena*

Everyone says forgiveness is a lovely idea, until they have something to forgive. *C. S. Lewis*

'I can forgive but I cannot forget' is only another way of saying 'I cannot forgive'. *Henry Ward Beecher*

A stiff apology is a second insult. *G. K. Chesterton*

Forgiveness needs to be accepted, as well as given, before it is complete. *C. S. Lewis*

Know all and you will pardon all. *Thomas à Kempis*

A guilty conscience is the mother of invention. *Carolyn Wells*

Do not think of the faults of others but of what is good in them and faulty in yourself. *St Teresa of Avila*

If we are bound to forgive an enemy, we are not bound to trust him. *Thomas Fuller*

~ Prayer ~

What men usually ask of God when they pray is that two and two not make four. *Source unknown*

There are few men who dare publish to the world the prayers they make to Almighty God. *Montaigne*

Is prayer your steering wheel or your spare tyre? *Corrie ten Boom*

Prayer is not trying to grab hold of God. Prayer is to recognize God coming to us. *Stephen Verney*

Prayer is the most important thing in my life. *Martin Luther*

The worst sin is prayerlessness. *P. T. Forsyth*

Prayer is conversation with God. *St Clement of Alexandria*

What's important is that God is so much part and parcel of life that spontaneous mental chat becomes second nature. *Cliff Richard*

Prayer makes the soul one with God. *Julian of Norwich*

Prayer is an exercise of the spirit, as thought is of the mind. *Mary F. Smith*

Prayer enlarges the heart until it is capable of containing God's gift of himself. *Mother Teresa*

We pray because we are made for prayer, and God draws us out by breathing himself in. *P. T. Forsyth*

Prayer does not change God, but it changes him who prays. *Sören Kirkegaard*

Prayer does not change God, it changes me. *C. S. Lewis*

Prayer gives a man the opportunity of getting to know a gentleman he hardly ever meets. I do not mean his maker but himself. *William Ralph Inge*

There are moments when, whatever be the attitude of the body, the soul is on its knees. *Victor Hugo*

In the sight of God no man can look at himself except when he is down on his knees. *François Mauriac*

I have been driven many times to my knees by the overwhelming conviction that I had nowhere else to go. My own wisdom, and that of all about me, seemed insufficient for the day. *Abraham Lincoln*

Tell God that you have, alas! no inclination to pray, and that you have dragged yourself to your knees. Still you will be welcome. *W. E. Sangster*

All the troubles of life come upon us because we refuse to sit quietly for a while each day in our rooms. *Blaise Pascal*

Really to pray is to stand to attention in the presence of the King and to be prepared to take orders from him. *Donald Coggan*

We are always in the presence of God, yet it seems to me that those who pray are in his presence in a very different way. *St Teresa of Avila*

You can set up an altar to God in your mind by means of prayer. *St John Chrysostom*

The more we receive in silent prayer, the more we can give in active life. *Malcolm Muggeridge*

Half an hour's listening is essential except when you are very busy. Then a full hour is needed. *St Francis de Sales*

I have so much to do that I must spend several hours in prayer before I am able to do it. *John Wesley*

In a single day I have prayed as many as a hundred times, and in the night almost as often. *St Patrick*

Perform all your actions with the life-giving breath of prayer. *Pope John XXIII*

Any concern too small to be turned into a prayer is too small to be made into a burden. *Corrie ten Boom*

In prayer, it is better to have a heart without words, than words without a heart. *John Bunyan*

A good prayer, though often used, is still fresh and fair in the eyes and ears of heaven. *Thomas Fuller*

In the Lord's Prayer, the first petition is for daily bread. No one can worship God or love his neighbour on an empty stomach. *Woodrow Wilson*

Only one petition in the Lord's Prayer has any condition attached to it; it is the petition for forgiveness. *William Temple*

The Lord's Prayer contains the sum total of religion and morals. *Arthur Wellesley, Duke of Wellington*

The Lord's Prayer may be committed to memory quickly, but it is slowly learnt by heart. *Frederick Denison Maurice*

Prayers travel faster when said in unison. *Latin proverb*

God ... dislikes our making prayer an excuse for neglecting the effort of doing good works. *Pope John Paul I*

Your cravings as a human animal do not become a prayer just because it is God you ask to attend to them. *Dag Hammarskjöld*

The servants of Christ are protected by invisible, rather than visible, beings. But if these guard you, they do so because they have been summoned by your prayers. *St Ambrose*

He prays best who does not know that he is praying. *St Antony of Padua*

The best prayers have often more groans than words. *John Bunyan*

We are silent at the beginning of the day because God should have the first word, and we are silent before going to sleep because the last word also belongs to God. *Dietrich Bonhoeffer*

Prayer should be the key of the day and the lock of the night. *Thomas Fuller*

~ Holy Communion ~

We eat the body of Christ that we may be able to be partakers of eternal life. *St Ambrose*

Holy Communion is the shortest and safest way to heaven. *Pope St Pius X*

As often as the Lord's blood is shed, it is poured out for the forgiveness of sins, so I ought to receive it always, that my sins may be always forgiven. *St Ambrose*

Breaking one bread, which is the medicine of immortality, the antidote against death which gives eternal life in Jesus. *Irenaeus*

The noblest sacrament ... is that wherein his body is really present. The Eucharist crowns all the other sacraments. *St Thomas Aquinas*

When it comes to the consecration of this venerable sacrament, the priest no longer uses his own language, but he uses the language of Christ. Therefore, the word of Christ consecrates this sacrament. *St Ambrose*

> 'Twas God the word that spake it,
> He took the Bread and brake it;
> And what the word did make it,
> That I believe and take it. *Elizabeth I*

You yourself both offer and are offered, you yourself both receive and are distributed, O Christ our God. *St John Chrysostom*

It is the mystery of yourselves that is laid on the Lord's table; it is the mystery of yourselves that you receive. To that which you are, you answer 'Amen', and in answering you assent. For you hear the words 'the body of Christ', and you reply 'Amen'. *St Augustine of Hippo*

This food satisfies the hunger of the devout heart. *St Thomas Aquinas*

If you have received well, you are what you have received. *St Augustine of Hippo*

The proper effect of the Eucharist is the transformation of man into God. *St Thomas Aquinas*

I don't think it far-fetched to draw a comparison between making love and making Eucharist. Perhaps the one reflects the other, the one a personal focus, the other a corporate focus, for the generating of love in the world ... After all, at the heart of each are the statements of person to person, and of God to the community of persons, 'You matter to me' and 'I am willing to die for you.' *Jim Cotter*

The name of the feast explains the reason for it; it is called by the Greek name for love [*agape*]. *Quintus Tertullian*

There are many mothers who after the pains of childbirth give their children to strangers to nurse. But Christ could not bear his children to be fed by others. He feeds us himself with his own blood. *St John Chrysostom*

A mother may feed her child with her own milk, but our precious mother Jesus feeds us with himself, and does it with great courtesy and tenderness, in feeding us with the blessed sacrament that is the precious food of life. *Julian of Norwich*

The Mass and the Eucharist are not only the centre of Christian worship, they are also the centre of Christian merry-making. *Eric Gill*

Wherever the sacred Host is to be found, there is the living God, there is your Saviour, as real as when he was living and talking in Galilee and Judea. *Charles de Foucauld*

In the noise and clutter of my kitchen, while several persons are at the same time calling for different things, I possess God in as great tranquillity as if I were upon my knees at the Blessed Sacrament. *Brother Lawrence*

~ Death and Bereavement ~

Dying

I lay all my actions before God who shall judge them and to whom I have consecrated them. *Blaise Pascal*

The difference is that we Europeans accept we've all got to die of something or other. Americans think that death is a calamity for which you can sue somebody. *Jonathan Miller*

There is a remedy for everything but death, which will be sure to lay us out flat at some time or other. *Cervantes*

Death is the greatest kick of all – that's why they save it till last. *A piece of graffiti in Los Angeles, 1982*

It's not that I'm afraid to die. I just don't want to be there when it happens. *Woody Allen in* Without Feathers *(1976)*

On the plus side, death is one of the few things that can be done as easily lying down. *Woody Allen in* Getting Even *(1972)*

The foolish fear death as the greatest of evils, the wise desire it as a rest after labours and the end of ills. *St Ambrose*

Men fear death as children fear to go in the dark; and as that natural fear in children is increased with tales, so is the other. *Francis Bacon*

When I look on all these worries I remember the story of the old man who said on his deathbed that he had had a lot of trouble in his life, most of which never happened. *Winston Churchill*

It is death and not what comes after death, that men are generally afraid of. *Samuel Butler*

It may be that the day of judgement will dawn tomorrow; in that case, we shall gladly stop working for a better future. But not before. *Dietrich Bonhoeffer*

Death is the great adventure, beside which moon landings and space trips pale into insignificance. *Joseph Bayly*

It matters not how a man dies, but how he lives. *Samuel Johnson*

My bags are packed and I am ready to go. *Pope John XXIII*

I am ready to meet my Maker. Whether my Maker is prepared for the ordeal of meeting me is another matter. *Winston Churchill on his seventy-fifth birthday*

If after I depart this vale, you ever remember me and have thought to please my ghost, forgive some sinner and wink your eye at some homely girl. *Henry L. Mencken*

I am able to follow my own death step by step. Now I move softly towards the end. *Pope John XXIII, a day or so before his death*

In my end is my beginning. *Mary Queen of Scots*

God bless you, my dear! *Samuel Johnson (his last words)*

Bereavement

The true way to mourn the dead is to take care of the living who belong to them. *Edmund Burke*

Grief is itself a medicine. *William Cowper*

Sorrow makes us all children again, destroys all differences in intellect. *Ralph Waldo Emerson*

Death is but crossing the world, as friends do the sea. *William Penn*

Death is like an airplane taking off. *Malcolm de Chazal*

Death is nothing at all ... I have only slipped away into the next room. *Henry Scott Holland*

We should not mourn for our brethren who have been freed from the world by the divine summons, since we know that they are not lost but gone on ahead. *St Cyprian*

There is nothing innocent or good that dies and is forgotten: let us hold to that faith or none. *Charles Dickens*

The final heartbeat for the Christian is not the mysterious conclusion to a meaningless existence. It is, rather, the grand beginning to a life that will never end. *James Dobson*

Death is but a sharp corner near the beginning of life's procession down eternity. *John Ayscough*

What is death at most? It is a journey for a season: a sleep longer than usual. *St John Chrysostom*

Death is the supreme festival on the road to freedom. *Dietrich Bonhoeffer*

Here in this world he bids us come, there in the next he shall bid us welcome. *John Donne*

And life is eternal and love is immortal, and death is only a horizon, and a horizon is nothing save the limit of our sight. *William Penn*

So he passed over, and all the trumpets sounded for him on the other side. *John Bunyan*

Funerals

Taking trouble over a funeral, giving dignified burial, having a grand funeral procession: all this is more to comfort the living than to be of use to the dead. *St Augustine of Hippo*

A damn good funeral is still one of our best and cheapest acts of theatre. *Gwyn Thomas*

Why should we wear black for the guests of God? *John Ruskin*

At death, if at any time, we see ourselves as we are, and display our true characters. *R. H. Benson*

Any man's death diminishes me because I am involved in mankind and therefore never send to hear for whom the bell tolls: it tolls for me. *John Donne*

If you don't go to people's funerals, they won't come to yours. *Anonymous*

The Future Life

See also 'Heaven', p. 91

I have never seen what to me seemed an atom of proof that there is a future life. And yet – I am strongly inclined to expect one. *Mark Twain*

It is impossible that anything so natural, so necessary, and so universal as death should ever have been designed by Providence as an evil to mankind. *Jonathan Swift*

I cannot conceive that God could make such a species as the human merely to live and die on this earth. If I did not believe in a future state, I should believe in no God. *John Adams*

Surely God would not have such a being as man … to exist only for a day! No, no, man was made for immortality. *Abraham Lincoln*

~ Heaven ~

I find heaven is on earth. I am stunned by the beauty of a blade of grass... If there is a heaven then I will consider it a bonus. *Spike Milligan*

Heaven means to be one with God. *Confucius*

Wherever the bounds of beauty, truth and goodness are advanced there the kingdom comes. *Donald Coggan*

All the way to heaven is heaven. *St Catherine of Siena*

Love of heaven is the only way to heaven. *John Henry Newman*

If you do not wish for his kingdom, don't pray for it. But if you do, you must do more than pray for it; you must work for it. *John Ruskin*

He who created us without our help will not save us without our consent. *St Augustine of Hippo*

Heaven is not to be looked upon only as the reward, but as the natural effect of a religious life. *Joseph Addison*

I have no liking for any other heaven than Jesus, who will be my joy when I come there. *Julian of Norwich*

My idea of heaven is eating pâté de foie gras to the sound of trumpets. *Sydney Smith*

When I get to heaven, I shall see three wonders there. The first wonder will be to see many there whom I did not expect to see; the second wonder will be to miss many people who I did expect to see; the third and greatest of all will be to find myself there. *John Newton*

If you're not allowed to laugh in heaven, I don't want to go there. *Martin Luther*

Whether the angels play only Bach praising God I am not quite sure. I am sure however that *en famille* they play Mozart. *Karl Barth*

Gratitude is heaven itself. *William Blake*

The main object of religion is not to get a man into heaven; but to get heaven into him. *Thomas Hardy*

He that will enter into paradise must come with the right key. *Thomas Fuller* (He that will enter paradise must have a good key. *George Herbert*)

God hath given to man a short time here upon earth, and yet upon this short time eternity depends. *Jeremy Taylor*

Heaven will be the endless portion of every man who has heaven in his soul. *Henry Ward Beecher*

I would not give one moment of heaven for all the joys and riches of the world, even if it lasted for thousands and thousands of years. *Martin Luther*

In heaven, they may bore you. In hell, you will bore them. *Katharine Whitehorn*

The doors of heaven and hell are adjacent and identical: both green, both beautiful. *Nicos Kazantzakis*

Many might go to heaven with half the labour they go to hell. *Ben Jonson*

Hell is full of the talented, but heaven of the energetic. *St Jeanne Françoise de Chantal*

Can there be paradise for any while there is hell, conceived as an unending torment, for some? Each supposedly damned soul was born into the world as a mother's child, and paradise cannot be paradise for her if her child is in such a hell. *William Temple*

A world of saints and angels, a glorious world, the palace of God, the mountain of the Lord of Hosts, the heavenly Jerusalem, the throne of God and Christ, all these wonders, everlasting, all-precious, mysterious and incomprehensible, lie hid in what we see. *John Henry Newman*

Angels can fly because they take themselves lightly. *G. K. Chesterton*

I know as much about the afterlife as you do – nothing. I must wait and see. *William Ralph Inge*

~ Proverbs ~

A selection of genuinely anonymous sayings

He who leaves God out of his reckoning does not know how to count. *Italy*

God shuts one door in order to open a hundred doors. *Yugoslavia*

God could not be everywhere so he made mothers. *Judaism*

You worship God in your way and I'll worship him in his. *Ireland*

The universe is a thought from God. *Germany*

Many millions search for God and find him in their hearts. *Sikhism*

God never closed one gap without opening another. *Ireland*

Prayer is a cry of hope. *France*

If God lived on earth, people would break his windows. *Yiddish*

Move yourself and God will assist you. *Greece*

Pray to God but keep rowing to the shore. *Russia*

The fewer the words, the better the prayer. *Germany*

One word of thanks reaches up to heaven. *Japan*

When a man say him do not mind, then him mind. *West Indies*

The old forget, the young don't know. *Germany*

Mercy is better than vengeance. *Greece*

Truth rests alone with God, and a little bit with me. *Yiddish*

'For example' is not proof. *Yiddish*

Who lies for you will lie against you. *Russia*

Committee: a group that takes minutes and wastes hours. *United States of America, allegedly*

~ Author Index ~

Saints are listed by their first names

Eric S. Abbott (1838–1926), an Anglican clergyman who was headmaster of the City of London School and, later, a full-time writer. 29

Arthur R. Adams (1861–?) 31

George M. Adams (1878–1962) was an American newsman and columnist. 37

Henry Brooks Adams (1838–1918), a North American historian whose books included a nine-volume *History of the United States*. 46, 61, 62, 63

John Adams (1735–1826), the first Vice-President of the United States of America (to Washington) and subsequently its second President – from 1797–1801. He died on the fiftieth anniversary of the signing of the Declaration of Independence. 90

Joseph Addison (1672–1719), the son of a Dean of Lichfield, he was an English essayist and poet and an MP from 1708 until his death. He contributed regularly to the papers the *Spectator* and the *Tatler*. 26, 32, 36, 71, 72, 91

Aesop (*fl.* 550 BC) is said to have been a slave, and both ugly and deformed. In fact, he is probably a semi-legendary character and his fables the work of many authors. 68

Louisa May Alcott (1832–88) was an American novelist, especially of books for young girls, the most famous of which being *Little Women* (1868), which describes the daily lives of the four March sisters in their New England home. 27

Woody Allen (1935–) was born Allen Stewart Konigsberg in Brooklyn in New York City and has achieved fame as a screenwriter, director and actor. 1, 87

St Ambrose (*circa* 340–97), a Roman governor who became a Christian, was chosen as Bishop of Milan by popular acclaim and who baptized St Augustine. 19, 39, 40, 57, 58, 68, 75, 82, 84

Anselm of Canterbury (1033–1109) was an Italian monk who became Archbishop of Canterbury. 7

St Antony of Padua (1195–1231) was born Ferdinand de Bulboes in Portugal, hoped to find martyrdom in North Africa, but became a travelling (and fiery) preacher in Italy. 14, 16, 82

Aristotle (384–322 BC) was a philosopher, teacher and writer in Ancient Greece. When he was 17, he went to Athens to join the Academy, a school run by Plato, later becoming a teacher himself. His thoughts on what divides humans from animals form the basis of his most famous book *The Politics*. 7

Lord Asquith (1858–1928), the first Earl of Oxford and Asquith, was a barrister and Liberal politician becoming Prime Minister in 1908. He introduced the old age pension and National Insurance and led Britain during the early years of the First World War. 63

St Athanasius (*circa* 296–373) was Bishop of Alexandria and a writer who strongly emphasized the divinity of Jesus Christ. 26, 27

Wystan Hugh Auden (1907–73) was an English poet who fought in the Spanish Civil War and who emigrated to the United States in 1939, subsequently taking American citizenship. Unlike some of his earlier writing, his later work was written from a Christian standpoint. 35

St Augustine of Hippo (354–430), born in North Africa, once abandoned his Christian faith for an immoral life but later became a bishop. His writings influenced Christians for many centuries though many now reject such convictions as the idea that babies not baptized before they die will go to hell. 4, 7, 12, 16, 20, 21, 24, 31, 41, 42, 67, 71, 77, 78, 79, 85, 89, 91

Alfred Jules 'Freddie' Ayer (1910–89) was Professor of Logic at Oxford University and a well-known atheist. 2

John Ayscough (1858–1928) 89

Sir Francis Bacon (1521–1626), Baron Verulam, Viscount St Alban, was an English lawyer, philosopher, scientist and MP. He published a number of essays on subjects including truth, ambition and death. There is little satisfactory evidence to support the claim that he wrote Shakespeare's plays. 1, 2, 12, 49, 54, 57, 58, 63, 64, 72, 87

John Baillie (1886–1960), a Scottish theologian and professor of divinity who wrote a popular *Diary of Private Prayer*. 24

John Austin Baker (1928–) was the Anglican Bishop of Salisbury from 1982 until 1993. 9, 28

Honoré de Balzac (1799–1850) was a major French writer – producing about 100 novels, which he planned to link with interconnecting characters under the title *La Comédie humaine*. 52

William Barclay (1907–78), a Scottish writer, theologian, broadcaster and popular commentator on the New Testament. 21, 26, 29

Michael Barnes SJ (1947–) is a Roman Catholic priest who teaches theology and inter-religious relations at Heythrop College in London University. 7, 8

Sir James Matthew Barrie (1860–1937) is most famous for his play about Peter Pan, the boy who didn't want to grow up, but he wrote many other plays and novels now often dismissed for their sentimentality. 5, 9, 66, 77

Karl Barth (1886–1968), a very influential Swiss Protestant theologian who studied and taught in German universities until his opposition to Naziism led to his return to Switzerland. 5, 12, 92

Bernard Mannes Baruch (1870–1965) was a rich American financier and politician – and also a close friend of Winston Churchill. 38

St Basil the Great (330–79), Bishop of Caesarea (in modern Turkey), many of whose sermons and letters have survived. A founder of the Church in Eastern Europe, he has inspired many Russian Christians. 5, 56

Richard Baxter (1615–91) was a nonconformist pastor and writer. 47, 55, 70

Joseph Bayly was a twentieth-century American novelist. 88

Frederick Beck (1861–1935) 29

Wendy Beckett is an English nun who taught in South Africa, but returned to lead a contemplative life under the protection of a Carmelite monastery in Norfolk. A lifelong art lover and recognized art historian, she catapulted to fame as a television art pundit. 66

The Venerable Bede (*circa* 673–735), an English monk (from the age of seven) and historian, noted for his *Ecclesiastical History of the English People* and sometimes described as 'the father of English history'. 42, 46, 64

Henry Ward Beecher (1813–87), an American Congregational minister famed for his preaching, opposition to slavery and support of women's rights. 14, 20, 22, 54, 79, 92

Hilaire Belloc (1870–1953) was an Anglo-French writer (his full name being Joseph Hilaire Pierre Belloc) born near Paris who became an English MP and was famous for his children's verses (the *Cautionary Tales*) – but he also wrote history, travel books and fiction. 33

St Benedict (480–550), studied in Rome, became a hermit, acquired many followers, and founded monasteries including the famous one at Monte Cassino. Here he wrote his 'Rule' as a way of helping his monks live their lives. He is known as 'the father of western monasticism'. 22, 70

Alan Bennett (1934–) was born in the Yorkshire city of Leeds and has achieved fame as a dramatist and a somewhat lugubrious actor. 8, 14, 22, 68

Enoch Arnold Bennett (1867–1931), an English novelist whose works feature the 'five towns' of his native Potteries district in Staffordshire. 35

W. C. Bennett was an American clergyman. 75

Robert Hugh Benson (1871–1914) is remembered as an English Roman Catholic writer but he originally trained as a member of the Anglican Community of the Resurrection at Mirfield. 4, 22, 44, 53, 55, 61, 90

David Edward Bentley (1935–) became the Anglican Bishop of Gloucester in 1993. 28

St Bernard of Clairvaux (1091–1153), a French monk and founder of the Cistercian Order. A great advocate of the Second Crusade to Palestine, he enthused so many volunteers that they died of hunger before reaching the Holy Land. 5, 12, 16, 21, 41, 59, 64

Ambrose Bierce (1842–*circa* 1914), an American journalist and writer of sardonic short stories who disappeared mysteriously while fighting in Mexico. viii, 78

Sir William Blackstone (1723–1780) was Professor of Law at Oxford University and author of *Commentaries on the Laws of England*. 67

William Blake (1757–1827), an English engraver, poet and artist especially famous for his poem 'Jerusalem' and for his illustrations to the book of Job. 16, 36, 65, 76, 92

Jacob Boehme (1627–1704) was born of peasant parents in Germany, became a shoemaker but spent much of his time in meditation and wrote a number of mystical works – sometimes in less than accessible language. 74

St Bonaventure (*circa* 1221–74), an Italian friar and follower of St Francis of Assisi whose writings had a long-lasting impact. 17, 57

Dietrich Bonhoeffer (1905–45), a German Lutheran pastor and university lecturer who was imprisoned and then executed by the Nazis for his opposition to them. Many of his writings were published posthumously. 12, 13, 24, 28, 29, 42, 49, 50, 70, 75, 83, 88, 89

Corrie ten Boom (1892–1983), a Dutch woman who (with her sister Betsie) saved many Jews from the Nazis but they were eventually caught and sent to a concentration camp where they inspired many other prisoners. She (but not Betsie) survived to become a well-known writer and evangelist. 10, 23, 25, 65, 80, 82

Jacques Bénigne Bossuet (1627–1704), a French priest who became Bishop of Meaux, is chiefly remembered as a great preacher and philosopher. 21, 46, 68

Bertolt Brecht (1898–1956) was a German dramatist and director. After escaping from Naziism to America, he returned to East Berlin in 1949. 67

Robert Bridges (1844–1930) worked as a doctor in London, becoming rich enough to retire in 1882. He then concentrated on his poetry and became Poet Laureate in 1913. He was also interested in church music. 45

Craig Edward Moncrieff Brown (1957–) is an English columnist, humorist and journalist. 64

Robert Browning (1812–89) was self-educated and, from an early age, a poet. His most famous poem is probably 'The Pied Piper of Hamelin'. In 1846 he eloped to Italy with another poet, Elizabeth Barrett. 41

Lenny Bruce (1925–66) was born Leonard Alfred Schneider in New York and became famous as a satirical comedian. 31

Jean de la Bruyère (1645–96), a French essayist and moralist whose scathing maxims expose human wickedness and folly. 44

James Bryce (1838–1922) was a professor of law, held various political posts and wrote on a variety of subjects including a book on *The American Commonwealth*. 70

John Buchan (1875–1940) was the writer of many famous adventure novels who also served on the headquarters staff of the Army in the First World War and was Governor-General of Canada from 1935 until 1940. 1

John Bunyan (1628–88) English nonconformist preacher and author of *The Pilgrim's Progress*. 82, 83, 89

Julie Burchill (1959–) is an English journalist who came to prominence when writing for the *New Musical Express* and who has more recently been a regular columnist for the *Guardian*. 1, 26

Edmund Burke (1729–97), an Irish Protestant politician who fought for Catholic emancipation. 2, 32, 48, 49, 88

George Burns (1896–1996) was an American comedian, born in New York City. 64

Nicholas Murray Butler (1862–1947) was an American educator and Nobel Peace Prize winner who was president of Columbia University from 1901 until 1945. 68

Samuel Butler (1835–1902), the son of a Nottinghamshire clergyman who refused to enter the Church himself because of his doubts and who devoted himself to painting and writing. 64, 87

James Branch Cabell (1879–1958) was an American novelist, born in Virginia. 2

Helder Camara (1909–99), a Brazilian Roman Catholic archbishop who campaigned tirelessly on behalf of the poor of Latin America, speaking out against and so antagonizing various military dictators. 2

Albert Camus (1913–60) was born in Algeria and worked for the Resistance in France during the Second World War. A humanist, he often wrote about the 'absurdity' of life. 65

John Pierre Camus (1582–1652), French bishop. 9, 49, 56, 64

Thomas Carlyle (1795–1881) was a Scottish historian and essayist, his most famous work being *The History of the French Revolution* – which he wrote twice, the second time being after a fire, which destroyed the first manuscript. 11, 16, 37, 58, 63, 74

Dale Carnegie (1888–1955) from the American state of Missouri achieved fame as an author and promoter of self-improvement techniques. 45

Alexis Carrel (1873–1944), a French-born biologist, he worked in the United States and won a Nobel Prize for medicine for his work on the surgery of blood vessels. Later, he devoted himself to cancer work. 68

Jesus de Castro 56

St Catherine of Siena (1347–80) never learned to read or write but some 400 of the letters she dictated have survived. A mystic, she spent her short life working among the poor of Siena. 17, 41, 79, 91

Catherine the Great (1729–96) ruled Russia for 34 years from 1762, turning it into an influential power. She did much to improve education for girls and the care of the sick but often sided with the nobility over the serfs. 47

Jean Pierre de Caussade (1675–1751) was a French Jesuit writer, preacher and mystic. 14, 24

Miguel de Cervantes (1547–1616) is chiefly remembered for his creation of Don Quixote, the hero of the epic, comic (and sad) Spanish novel that bears his name. 8, 33, 56, 87

William Ellery Channing (1780–1842), a Congregationalist minister in Boston who preached against the doctrine of the Trinity and who, by 1820, was considered to be a Unitarian. 17

John Jay Chapman (1862–1933) was Harvard-educated. Reluctantly, he became a lawyer but turned to writing, becoming known as a somewhat crotchety critic and essayist who often wrote on literary and religious matters. 20, 62

Malcolm de Chazal (1902–81), a French writer and recluse who lived on the island of Mauritius and who, for a while, explored the occult but is best known for his collection of about 2,000 aphorisms. 88

Anton Pavlovich Chekhov (1860–1904), an influential and successful Russian playwright and writer of many short stories, which hint at the beauty and tragedy of life. 5, 38, 77

Earl of Chesterfield (Philip Dormer Stanhope) (1694–1773) was an MP before inheriting his earldom when he held many high political offices. Many writers were among his friends. 33, 45

Gilbert Keith Chesterton (1874–1936), an English writer and critic who converted to Roman Catholicism and is best known for his Father Brown detective stories. 6, 13, 17, 20, 23, 34, 38, 59, 60, 64, 67, 68, 72, 74, 79, 93

Sir Winston Churchill (1874–1965) entered Parliament as a Conservative in 1900, became a Liberal in 1904 and then held several cabinet posts, later rejoining the Conservatives. During the 1930s, his warnings of war were ignored but he was asked to become Prime Minister in 1940. His famous speeches did much to maintain British morale during the Second World War. 53, 61, 64, 87, 88

Marcus Tullius Cicero (106–43 BC) was a Roman orator, politician and philosopher. He supported but did not take part in the murder of Julius Caesar and was later put to death on Mark Antony's orders. 10, 75

St Clare of Assisi (*circa* 1194–1253) became a follower of St Francis and set up a companion order to the Franciscans – the 'Poor Clares'. Because she once 'saw' in her mind a service taking place in a church some way away, she was (in 1958) named patron saint of television. 75

Kenneth Mackenzie Clark (1903–83) was a British art historian who later became famous as the presenter of a definitive 1969 television series, *Civilisation*. He was also made a life peer that year. 35

St Clement of Alexandria (*circa* 150–215) was of Greek origin and became a teacher in Alexandria, later fleeing to Jerusalem to avoid persecution. 12, 39, 71, 73, 80

Frederick Donald Coggan (1909–2000) was Archbishop of Canterbury from 1974 to 1980. An evangelical, he was also much concerned with social issues. 12, 61, 81, 91

Samuel Taylor Coleridge (1772–1834), an English Romantic poet and friend of Wordsworth, he is most famous for his 'Rime of the Ancient Mariner' but was also a Unitarian preacher – and much addicted to opium. 19, 45, 63

John Churton Collins (1848–1908) wrote much literary criticism and argued for the recognition of English literature as a university subject. 34

Confucius (551–479 BC), a travelling teacher of young noblemen in ancient China whose writings were written down in a collection known as *The Analects*. 91

Joseph Conrad (1857–1924) was a Polish-born novelist, resident in Britain, whose books draw on his earlier experiences as a seaman. 47

John Calvin Coolidge (1872–1933), a laconic Republican, he served as Governor of Massachusetts and subsequently as President of the United States of America from 1923 to 1929. 74

Thomas Corbishley (1903–76) was a Roman Catholic priest and distinguished member of the Society of Jesus. 16

James England (Jim) Cotter (1942–) is an English Anglican priest and writer on gay issues. 85

William Cowper (1731–1800) was a popular English poet whose life was marked by an evangelical fervour and periods of melancholia. He collaborated on the writing of the *Olney Hymns*. 9, 17, 18, 88

Oliver Cromwell (1599–1658) viewed the English Civil War as a religious fight and a way of bringing 'true godliness' to England. He fought for the execution of King Charles I and became Lord Protector and ruler of England from 1653. 10

St Cyprian (*circa* 200–58) became Bishop of Carthage just two years after his conversion from paganism but suffered persecution from the Romans and became the first martyr-bishop of Africa. 31, 89

St Cyril of Jerusalem (*circa* 315–86) was Bishop of Jerusalem from 349 and did much to establish it as a centre of pilgrimage. 29, 39, 40, 78

Dante Alighieri (1265–1321), an Italian poet from Florence, especially famous for his three-part epic poem *La Divina Commedia* describing his journey through hell, purgatory and heaven. 10

Charles Robert Darwin (1809–82) is best known for his theory of evolution by natural selection: 'the survival of the fittest'. Born in Shrewsbury, England, his book *The Origin of Species* caused an ongoing uproar when published in 1859 for apparently contradicting Genesis. 36

Hans Denck (*circa* 1495–1527) was a German reformist but an opponent of Lutheranism. 9

Charles Dickens (1812–70), the great Victorian novelist, drew on many of his childhood experiences of poverty for his stories which drew attention to many of the scandalous working conditions of nineteenth-century Britain. 27, 53, 89

Benjamin Disraeli, Earl of Beaconsfield (1804–81) was Jewish, married into wealth, found happiness with his wife, and rose through the ranks of the Conservative party (despite his background) to become a great reforming Prime Minister who supported the expansion of the Empire and who flattered Queen Victoria. 63

James Dobson (1936–) 89

John Donne (1572–1631) had careers in the law and as a 'gentleman adventurer' before being ordained and becoming Dean of St Paul's in London. He is now chiefly remembered as a poet. 27, 30, 39, 77, 89, 90

Fyodor Dostoyevsky (1821–81), one of the great Russian novelists, he was tormented by debt and a hater of religious obsessiveness but respected both in his own country and abroad for his writing. 12, 17, 34, 66

John Dryden (1631–1700), an important English dramatist and poet, he was appointed Poet Laureate – a post he lost when he converted to Roman Catholicism. 34

Meister Eckhart (*circa* 1260–1327), a German Dominican monk and mystic highly regarded in his own time for his preaching. 8, 17, 26, 56, 74

Mary Baker Eddy (1821–1910) was the American founder of the Christian Science movement. She believed that matter was subservient to the mind and that all physical ailments could be overcome by 'spiritual power'. 11, 69

Albert Einstein (1879–1955) was born German and became one of the world's greatest physicists, his theories directly or indirectly leading to the development of lasers, television, computers and space travel. He strongly opposed the Nazis, moved to America in 1933 and campaigned against nuclear weapons after 1945. 5

George Eliot, the pen name of **Marian Evans Cross** (1819–80), who was a journalist and novelist who published her books under a pseudonym as she thought male writers were taken more seriously. 35, 55

Thomas Stearns Eliot (1888–1965) was American-born but took British citizenship in 1927. A poet, critic and dramatist, he moved from agnosticism to Anglo-Catholicism and his faith is reflected in, especially, his poetry. 4, 11, 34, 44

Elizabeth I (1533–1603), Queen of England from 1558 until her death. Clever, stubborn and not fond of spending money, she nevertheless won people's affection. She was a great defender of the Church of England. 84

Ralph Waldo Emerson (1803–82) was born in Boston, Massachusetts, the son of a Unitarian minister. He became a popular lecturer but thought of himself primarily as a poet. In his controversial writings, he placed much emphasis on instinct and intuition. 32, 37, 45, 46, 47, 55, 60, 74, 77, 88

Epictetus (*circa* 55–135), a Greek stoic philosopher, who preached that we should try to escape 'the slavery of desire'. 65, 74

Epicurus (341–270 BC), a Greek epicurean philosopher – the Epicurean system of beliefs being a rival to Stoicism – who preached moderation in physical pleasures. 78

Frederick William Faber (1814–63), an English convert to Roman Catholicism and founder of the London Oratory, he also wrote many still-popular hymns. 23

George Farquhar (1678–1707) was originally a soldier but then turned to acting, giving up this second career when he accidentally wounded another actor. He then became a playwright and his comedies are distinctive for their realism and good nature. 62

Austin Farrer (1904–68) was an English theologian, philosopher and author. 14, 32

François Fénelon (1651–1715), a French priest and mystic, he became a royal tutor until religious controversy resulted in his exile from court and a quieter life as Archbishop of Cambrai. 58, 75

Henry Fielding (1707–54) wrote for the stage, became a lawyer and then took up writing novels, the greatest of which is the comic epic, *Tom Jones*. His published pamphlets indicate a wise and liberal mind. 58

Henry Ford (1863–1947) built his first car in 1893, starting the American Ford Motor Company in 1903. He became famous for inventing the 'production line', among his earlier models being the Model T and the Tin Lizzie: 'You can have any colour you like, so long as it's black.' 60, 71

P. Fontaine 51

Peter Taylor Forsyth (1848–1921) was a liberal Scottish Congregational pastor and theologian. 19, 22, 23, 27, 49, 80

Harry Emerson Fosdick (1878–1969), a North American Baptist minister, he worked for 20 years in New York and his books reflect his liberal evangelical stance. 5, 10, 77

Charles de Foucauld (1858–1916), a once dissolute French explorer who found Catholicism, became (for a while) a Trappist monk and was eventually assassinated in the Sahara. His 'rules of life' continue to be a source of inspiration to many. 21, 86

George Fox (1624–91), the English founder of the Society of Friends whose followers are often called Quakers. A great traveller, his preaching often landed him in prison. 27, 31

Matthew Fox (1940–) is a North American Roman Catholic priest and mystic in the tradition of Meister Eckhart. 29

Anatole France (1844–1924) was a French writer, a Nobel prize-winner and a tolerant and non-dogmatic philosopher who suggested 'beliefs are only opinions'. 35

St Francis of Assisi (1181–1226) renounced his family wealth, embraced poverty and eventually was allowed to establish an order of friars – the Franciscans. His love of God, of his fellow human beings and of all creatures have made him one of the best-loved saints. 21, 24

St Francis (François) de Sales (1567–1622), a Catholic Bishop of Geneva and writer who converted many Swiss Calvinists to Catholicism. 17, 33, 41, 46, 48, 70, 71, 81

Viktor Frankl (1905–97) was a Viennese psychologist and psychiatrist. With his wife and parents he was interned by the Nazis in a concentration camp during the Second World War but survived to become a noted university professor and philosopher whose books include *The Doctor and the Soul* and *Man's Search for Meaning*. 69

Benjamin Franklin (1706–90) was a North American statesman and scientist, popularly remembered for flying his kite during a thunderstorm – in an attempt to prove lightning was a giant electrical spark. 25, 57, 68

Sigmund Freud (1856–1939) was an Austrian Jew who became a doctor and who changed the way we think about ourselves. His central belief was that present strange behaviour was linked to troubles buried in our memories. 78

Elizabeth Fry (1780–1845), the daughter of an English Quaker banker who married into the chocolate-making Fry family who were strict Quakers. The mother of nine children, she became a 'minister' and devoted herself to prison reform. 22

Stephen Fry (1957–) is an English wit, writer and actor. 60

David Otis Fuller (?–1988) was a sometimes controversial American pastor and Bible scholar, director of the Which Bible Society. 25

Margaret Fuller (1810–50), born in Massachusetts, was a writer and pioneer campaigner for women's rights who died with her husband in a shipwreck. 55

Richard Buckminster Fuller (1895–1983) had the distinction of being twice expelled from Harvard. An engineer, architect and inventor, he worked to lower the cost of building houses and vehicles. 5

Thomas Fuller (1608–61), an English priest and witty writer whose histories chronicle the English Civil War, the development of Cambridge University and the English Church. 1, 45, 47, 49, 58, 69, 73, 79, 82, 83, 92

Monica Furlong (1930–2003) was an English writer and feminist. 57, 78

Galen (*circa* 130–201) was a Greek physician, appointed surgeon to the gladiators. His books became the definitive medical textbooks of the Classical, Latin and Arabic worlds for nearly 1,400 years. 69

André Gide (1869–1951) was a French novelist, dramatist and critic. 64

Eric Gill (1882–1940), an English sculptor and engraver who developed deep religious convictions after his conversion to Roman Catholicism. 85

James M. Gillis was, in the 1930s, a popular Catholic writer, lecturer and Christian apologist. 11

Johann Wolfgang von Goethe (1749–1832), Germany's most famous poet and dramatist, especially famous for his retelling of the Faust legend. 37, 42, 51, 54

Oliver Goldsmith (1728–74), the son of an Irish clergyman, he was himself rejected for ordination and turned to medicine. He took up writing: poetry, articles and, eventually, the plays for which he is remembered – notably *She Stoops to Conquer*. 64

Barrie Morris Goldwater (1909–98), a Phoenix-born businessman and right-wing politician, he supported the anti-Communist activities of Joseph McCarthy. 48

Billy Graham (1918–) is a North American evangelist who, since 1943, has undertaken many extensive preaching tours both inside and outside the United States. These crusades are run by his business organization and he has been friend to many Presidents. 14, 18, 23, 24, 36, 49, 57, 58, 59

Henry Graham Greene (1904–91) was an English novelist and dramatist who converted to Roman Catholicism. That faith was subsequently often a dominant theme in his writing. 2

Pope St Gregory I (540–604), often known as Gregory the Great. He did much to reform the church and, famously, sent St Augustine to convert England to Christianity. His interest in liturgy led to plainsong becoming known as 'Gregorian chant'. 19

Joyce Grenfell (1910–79) was an English comic actress, specializing in 'gawky' roles; the writer and performer of many monologues, writer, broadcaster and devout Christian Scientist. 20, 75

Dag Hjalmar Agne Carl Hammarskjöld (1905–61) was a Swedish statesman and Secretary-General of United Nations who was killed in a plane crash while on a truce-making mission. 6, 18, 44, 70, 75, 82

Thomas Hardy (1840–1928) set his often pessimistic novels in his native Dorsetshire – which he renamed Wessex – and suffered an unhappy first marriage. When his public turned against him, he concentrated on writing poetry. 92

Michael Geoffrey Hare Duke (1925–) was the Scottish Episcopal Bishop of St Andrews from 1969 until 1994 and also a hymn writer. 28

Richard Douglas Harries (1936–) became Bishop of Oxford in 1987 and is widely known as a broadcaster and author. 32

Sidney J. Harris was a twentieth-century American writer and author of *Winners and Losers*, an introduction to ethical decision-making. 24

Robert Stephen Hawker (1804–75), an opium smoker and country parson, is credited with having established the modern tradition of harvest festivals when Vicar of Morwenstow in the English county of Cornwall. 30

Franz Josef Haydn (1732–1809) was an Austrian composer, sometimes described as 'the father of the symphony'. Besides his symphonies, operas and string quartets, he wrote much church music. 74

William Hazlitt (1778–1830), the son of a Unitarian minister; essayist, critic and journalist who worked on various London newspapers. 34, 36, 68

Denis Healey (1917–) was for 40 years a Labour MP, serving for 33 years on Labour's Front Bench, notably as Chancellor of the Exchequer. In 1992 he was created Baron Healey of Riddlesden. 63

Heinrich Heine (1797–1856), a German poet born of Jewish parents but baptized a Christian in 1835, he is most famous as a lyric poet but he also wrote on politics. 51

Joseph Heller (1923–) is a noted American writer famous especially for his novel *Catch-22*. 63

Charles R. Hembree 63

Matthew Henry (1662–1714) was an English nonconformist preacher. 56

Sir Alan Patrick Herbert (1890–1971) was an English MP and writer of light verse, contributing regularly to *Punch* from 1910 onwards. 64

George Herbert (1593–1633), an Anglican priest regarded as one of the Church of England's greatest poets, he also wrote *A Priest to the Temple*, which contains 'plain, prudent useful rules for the country parson'. 2, 3, 8, 46, 76, 92

Theodore M. Hesburgh (1917–) is an American Roman Catholic priest and President of Notre Dame University teacher. He also served on the US Civil Rights commission. 53

Leonard Hodgson (1889–1969) was an Anglican priest, theologian and lecturer at Oxford University. 14

Canon Henry Scott Holland (1847–1918), a liberal high churchman, was an English theologian and preacher whose ideals were shattered by the horrors of the First World War. 89

Michael Hollings won an MC as a soldier in the Second World War, became a Roman Catholic priest and writer and was a famous chaplain to Oxford University. 9

Richard Frederick Holloway (1933–) was Primus of the Episcopal Church of Scotland from 1992 until 2000 who became well known for his radical views. 10

Oliver Wendell Holmes (1809–94) was an American author and physician, now best known for his humorous essays and verses. 68

Bob Hope (1903–) was born in Eltham in south London but was raised in Ohio, becoming an American citizen in 1920. Beginning in vaudeville, he became one of the great comedians of the twentieth century. 51, 65

Herbert Clark Hoover (1874–1964), President of the United States of America at the time of the Great Depression from 1929 to 1932. 49, 60

Elbert G. Hubbard (1856–1915) was an American schoolteacher, printer, editor and lecturer. 45, 47, 77

Frank McKinney ('Kin') Hubbard (1868–1930) was born in Ohio into an eccentric family. He became a journalist but is chiefly remembered as creator of a cartoon character Abe Martin, 'a home-cured philosopher'. 67

Victor Marie Hugo (1802–85) was a French writer who published his first novel at the age of 17. He also wrote plays and poems but two of his most famous works are the novels *Notre-Dame de Paris* (with its hunchback) and *Les Misérables*. 36, 73, 81

David Hume (1711–76), Scottish philosopher conveniently described as an atheist, but whose writings on religion are both provocative and perceptive. 4

Aldous Leonard Huxley (1894–1963) was the English author of a number of satirical novels including *Brave New World*. 63

St Ignatius Loyola (1491–1556), the Spanish founder of the Roman Catholic Society of Jesus whose members are known as Jesuits. 33

William Ralph Inge (1860–1954), Dean of St Paul's Cathedral in London and author of various philosophical and devotional books. Because of his comments on modern life, he was nicknamed 'the Gloomy Dean'. 4, 5, 8, 20, 33, 34, 61, 81, 93

Irenaeus (130–202) was a Bishop of Lyons who may have come there from Myrna, which is now part of Turkey. 16, 84

Holbrook Jackson (1874–1948) was an English writer and critic. 64

Clive James (1939–) is an Australian-born critic, poet, author and television personality. 30

St Jeanne Françoise de Chantal (1572–1641) was the wife of a French baron who was killed in a hunting accident. With the help of St Francis de Sales, she founded an order of nuns, turning her convent into a hospital during a time of plague. 92

Thomas Jefferson (1743–1826), President of the United States of America and one of the principal writers of the Declaration of Independence. 38

James Jennings (1854–1920) 19

St Jerome (*circa* 341–420) was born in France, educated in Rome, lived in the Syrian desert and eventually settled in Bethlehem. He is remembered especially for his Latin translation of the bible, the Vulgate. 19, 20, 33, 39, 41, 42, 45, 46, 57

Jerome Klapka Jerome (1859–1927) was an English novelist and playwright now remembered almost exclusively for his comic masterpiece *Three Men in a Boat*. 68

Douglas Jerrold (1803–57) was an English journalist, humorist and playwright, famous especially for his nautical melodrama *Black-Eyed Susan*. 30

John Jewell (1522–71) was Bishop of Salisbury. 33

St John Chrysostom (*circa* 347–407) trained as a lawyer before becoming a monk and later a priest. He preached in Antioch (Chrysostom is Greek for 'golden mouth') before becoming Bishop of Constantinople. 19, 20, 27, 29, 32, 38, 57, 61, 75, 77, 81, 84, 85, 89

St John of Avila (1500–69) was a mystic and influential priest who preached throughout the Andalusia region of Spain. 75

John of Carpathos (seventh century) was a Greek monk. 17, 72

St John of the Cross (1542–91), a Spanish mystic and monk who was embroiled in (and suffered on account of) the dissent between branches of the Carmelite

Order, is now remembered as the author of the classic *Dark Night of the Soul*. 9, 17, 24, 28, 42, 43, 69

St John of Damascus (*circa* 675–749) lived in a monastery near Jerusalem and wrote many books, notably the *Fount of Wisdom* which outlines the beliefs of the Orthodox Church. 7

Pope John XXIII (Angelo Giuseppe Roncalli) (1881–1963) summoned the Second Vatican Council and gave it the task of renewing the spiritual life of the church. He did much to encourage relations with other churches. Much loved, he was also a shrewd administrator. 33, 34, 37, 49, 53, 67, 82, 88

Pope John Paul I (1912–78), a man of great personal simplicity, he died quite unexpectedly just five weeks after being elected Pope. 82

Pope John Paul II (1920–) was born near Kraków in Poland and was a published poet and playwright who in 1946 became a priest. He was elected Pope in 1978, the first non-Italian Pope since 1523. 28, 32, 41, 55, 65, 78

Samuel Johnson (1709–84), the great English writer and lexicographer who published his *Dictionary* in 1755, edited the magazines the *Rambler* and the *Idler*; was a great conversationalist and is remembered through the biography written by his friend James Boswell. 2, 22, 31, 50, 51, 53, 57, 58, 60, 61, 62, 67, 69, 72, 78, 88

Franklin P. Jones 53

Ben Jonson (1573–1637) was a bricklayer, soldier and actor before writing the plays that made his name. His targets were human greed, gullibility and pride. 92

Joseph Joubert (1754–1824), a French writer and moralist who lived through the French Revolution, he is chiefly remembered for his *Pensées* or 'Thoughts'. 9

Benjamin Jowett (1817–93) was an Anglican priest, scholar and Professor of Greek at Oxford University. 6

John Henry Jowett (1841–1923) was an English Congregational preacher. 10, 58

Julian of Norwich (1342– sometime after 1413) lived in a cell in St Julian's Church, Norwich, in eastern England, and received a series of visions which she described in her influential book *Revelations of Divine Love*. 73, 80, 85, 91

Decimus Junius Juvenal (*circa* 60–130) was a Roman satirical poet. His views on Jews and women were, at best, venomous but he did attack much that was vicious in the society in which he lived. 35

Franz Kafka (1883–1924), an Austrian-Jewish novelist, little of whose work was published before his death. Many have noted a recurring theme in his work: our struggle to establish a relationship with God. 36

Nicos Kazantzakis (1883–1957) was a Greek author, poet and dramatist best known for a novel which, in English, was called *Zorba the Greek*. 92

Helen Keller (1880–1968) was born in Alabama and achieved success as a writer and scholar despite being blind, deaf and almost mute. 48, 70

John Kelman 31

Thomas à Kempis (1379–1471) was born near Cologne in Germany, became an Augustinian monk and wrote many books, notably *The Imitation of Christ*, which traces the progress of the Christian soul to perfection. 10, 25, 41, 46, 66, 69, 78, 79

John Fitzgerald Kennedy (1917–63), one of nine children, won political success with the help of his extensive family, being elected President of the United States of America in 1960. He was assassinated by a sniper's bullet in Dallas, Texas, in November 1963. 10

Jean Kerr (1923–2003) was an American author and playwright, several of whose comedies achieved success on Broadway. 53

Søren Kierkegaard (1813–55) was a Danish theologian who was constantly concerned with the individual's search for God and Christ although he rejected belief in the historical incarnation. 25, 80

Edward King (1829–1910) was Bishop of Lincoln. 33

Charles Kingsley (1819–75), an English clergyman, novelist and reformer, he was founder of the Christian Socialist Movement and one of the first clerics to support Darwin's theories of evolution. 5, 48, 69, 75

Rudyard Kipling (1865–1936) was born to British parents in Bombay in India. After school in England, he returned to India where he wrote *The Jungle Book, The Just So Stories* and *Kim* – books that have had an enduring appeal for children and adults. 34

John Knox (*circa* 1513–72) was a Scottish reformer, chaplain to the English King Edward VI and, after a period in Geneva, a leader of the Protestant movement in his home country. 10

La Rochefoucauld (1613–80) was a French duke and something of a cynic but his 'maxims' remorselessly analyse human nature. 36, 38, 45, 51, 52, 65, 72

William Laroe 31

Brother Lawrence, originally Nicholas Herman (*circa* 1605–91) was born in Lorraine in France. He became a soldier and then a footman, entering a Carmelite community in about 1649 and remaining there until his death. His letters have had a widespread influence. 14, 25, 74, 86

John Lawrence was, in the middle years of the twentieth century, a prominent ecumenist and editor of the influential *Christian Newsletter*. 21

Gustave Le Bon (1841–1931) was a French psychologist and philosopher. 16

Stanislaw Jerzy Lec (1909–66) 8

Graham Leonard (1921–) became a Roman Catholic priest in 1994 after having been the Anglican Bishop of London from 1981 until 1991. 33

Clive Staples Lewis (1898–1963), a lecturer at both Oxford and Cambridge Universities, he is remembered for his children's Christian allegories about the land of Narnia as well as for his religious writings for adults. 5, 7, 9, 23, 42, 46, 65, 66, 71, 74, 78, 79

Georg Christoph Lichtenberg (1742–99), a German professor of physics, wrote many essays and is noted for his satirical deflation of human pomposity. 36

Joseph Barber Lightfoot (1828–89) was an English biblical scholar, a professor of divinity at Cambridge University and, later, Bishop of Durham. 75

Abraham Lincoln (1809–65) was President of the United States of America during the American Civil War. His famous speech about democracy ('government of the people, by the people, for the people . . .') was made while dedicating a soldiers' cemetery after the battle of Gettysburg. 8, 23, 53, 81, 90

John L. Lincoln was an American evangelical businessman. 68

David Livingstone (1813–73) was a Scottish explorer and missionary who worked in Africa, seeking out the source of the Nile. It was in 1871 that the American journalist Henry M. Stanley sought him out in the midst of the continent, allegedly greeting him with the words, 'Doctor Livingstone, I presume?' 23

Henry Wadsworth Longfellow (1807–82), an American poet, is especially remembered for his poems 'Hiawatha' and 'Paul Revere's Ride'. 47

Martin Luther (1483–1546) was an Augustinian monk and priest. It was while lecturing at the German University of Wittenberg in 1517 that he nailed his 95 theses to various church doors, thus becoming a key figure in the Reformation. He gave up his monastic vows in 1524 in order to marry. 19, 20, 22, 29, 40, 53, 54, 66, 68, 70, 80, 91, 92

Sir James Mackintosh (1765–1832) was a Scot who worked in London as a journalist and, later, barrister and in Bombay as a judge. He returned to be an MP and wrote on history and philosophy. 59

Henry Manning (1808–92) came from an evangelical Protestant background, but turned his allegiance to 'high church' Anglicanism and, after ordination and marriage, to Roman Catholicism. On the death of his wife, he was ordained in that Church, soon becoming the second Archbishop of Westminster – and later, Cardinal. 33, 47

Karl Marx (1818–83) was a German whose pamphlet *The Communist Manifesto* led to his expulsion from Germany, France and Belgium. Settling in London, he developed his communist ideals including his belief in the abolition of private property. 1

Mary Queen of Scots (1542–89), Queen of Scotland, was executed as she was considered a threat to Queen Elizabeth I of England. 88

François Mauriac (1885–1970) was a French novelist and dramatist and also a fervent Roman Catholic preoccupied with the conflicts between Christian morality and human passions. 81

Frederick Denison Maurice (1805–72) was an English clergyman and writer with a strong social conscience. 27, 82

André Maurois (1885–1967) was a French writer often preoccupied with things English – writing books about Shelley, Disraeli and Byron as well as histories of England and the United States. 51

Henry Louis Mencken (1880–1956) was an American author, critic and journalist – often outspoken and sometimes prejudiced but an opponent of complacency. 2, 4, 34, 35, 60, 72, 88

Thomas Merton (1915–68) was a North American journalist who became a monk. His prolific writings (including his autobiographical *The Seven Storey Mountain*) did much to popularize Western spirituality. 6, 9, 26, 42

Jonathan Wolfe Miller (1934–) is a British theatre and opera director, writer, television presenter and, originally, medical doctor. 87

Spike Milligan (1918–2002) (real name: Terence Milligan) achieved fame by writing and appearing in the radio comedy series *The Goon Show* – the pressure of which task caused him much mental anguish. He was also a great television comic, humorous poet and writer. 91

John Milton (1608–74) is often said to have been England's second greatest poet (after Shakespeare). He supported Cromwell and the Puritans during England's Civil War and is chiefly honoured for his great biblical epic poem *Paradise Lost*. 1, 62

Molière (Jean Baptiste Poquelin) (1622–73) left home to become an actor with a French touring company for whom he wrote many witty and often satirical plays. They were eventually given a permanent theatre in Paris by the king. 45

Michel Eyquem Montaigne (1533–92), a member of a well-to-do French family, is remembered for his essays in which he discusses religious and moral questions with tolerant scepticism. 80

Baron de Montesquieu (1689–1755), otherwise Charles de la Brède; a French nobleman and philosopher and a respected commentator on society and politics. 67

Dwight L. Moody (1837–99), a North American evangelist who believed in the literal truth of the Bible, he undertook many preaching tours accompanied by the musician Ira David Sankey. The hymns and songs they used appeared in *The Moody and Sankey Hymn Book*. 15, 20, 35, 41

The Reverend Dr Colin Morris (1929–) is a British Methodist preacher and broadcaster. 11, 50

Thomas Malcolm Muggeridge (1903–90), a witty and perceptive English journalist who became a television pundit, often pontificating on religious matters. 65, 81

Alfred de Musset (1810–57), French poet, dramatist and aristocratic dandy who suffered bouts of pessimism and depression but whose writing often sparkles with wit and insight. 25

Ogden Nash (1902–71) was an American humorous poet whose work often appeared in the *New Yorker*. 54

Stephen Charles Neill (1900–84) was a classical scholar who taught in various universities and was consecrated bishop in 1931. He served in various dioceses in Asia and Africa. 12

Cardinal John Henry Newman (1801–90) was an Oxford Anglican vicar and the leader of the 'high church' Oxford Movement but, dissatisfied with the Church of England, he became a Roman Catholic, was priested and eventually made a cardinal in 1879. 2, 5, 10, 18, 26, 45, 46, 91, 93

John Newton (1725–1807) was an evangelical clergyman who became curate of Olney in the English county of Buckinghamshire where he collaborated with William Cowper on producing the *Olney Hymns*. 91

Joseph F. Newton (1878–1950) was a Texan clergyman and writer. Originally a Baptist, he later founded several non-sectarian churches and was eventually ordained into the Episcopalian Church. 44

Martin Niemoller (1892–1984) was a pastor in the German Lutheran who opposed the Nazi interference in the Church and was imprisoned in the Dachau concentration camp. After the war, he helped to re-establish the Church and became a president of the World Council of Churches. 29, 48, 78

Friedrich Wilhelm Nietzsche (1844–1900), the son of a German pastor who developed a contempt for Christianity, admired paganism and lauded the deeds of 'supermen' over 'the masses' (some of his ideas being adopted by the Nazis). His writings nevertheless are still a challenge to the believer. 1, 3, 8, 45, 46

John Keith Oliver (1935–) became Bishop of Hereford in 1990. 18

Origen (*circa* 185–254), an Alexandrian biblical scholar and writer, he was ordained priest in Jerusalem but found a spiritual home in Caesarea where he established a school. He was imprisoned and tortured in 250. 71, 77

Sir William Osler (1849–1919) was born in Canada, became a physician and professor of medicine at Oxford University. Besides medical works, he wrote a number of essays. 70

Thomas Paine (1737–1809) was an English political writer who went to America, and returned to write his most famous work, *The Rights of Man* – which resulted in his being forced to go to France to avoid prosecution. Later, he settled in America. 23

Blaise Pascal (1623–62) was a French theologian and mathematician who invented and patented an early calculator and also the syringe but he is best remembered for his *Pensées* or 'Thoughts' on the Christian religion. 1, 4, 5, 9, 18, 21, 25, 42, 50, 66, 74, 81, 87

St Patrick (*circa* 389–461), 'The Apostle of the Irish', may have been part Welsh and part Roman. He worked and preached throughout Ireland, the first country in the West outside the Roman Empire to hear the Christian message. Much of his life has been surrounded by myth and legend. 82

Cesare Pavese (1908–50) was an Italian poet and novelist who committed suicide after 20 years' 'intellectual loneliness'. 37, 61

Paul the Great (fourth century) was one of the desert fathers. 13

Norman Vincent Peale (1898–1993) was an American pastor and writer who was much in demand as a lecturer. 69

Charles Péguy (1873–1914) was a French Catholic writer and manager of a Paris bookshop, which became a centre for Christian Socialism. He joined the French army in 1914 and was killed in the Battle of Marne. 42, 59, 72

William Penn (1644–1718), born in Oxford, was a Quaker and was imprisoned in the Tower of London where he wrote *No Cross, No Crown*. Twelve years later, he left England for America, became a founding father of Pennsylvania, which he developed as a colony that supported freedom of conscience for all monotheistic believers. 13, 28, 67, 73, 88, 89

Samuel Pepys (1633–1703) was an English civil servant who is famous for his detailed diary, which describes the London scene and especially both the Great Plague and the Great Fire. 56, 71

John Bertram Phillips (1906–82) was a Church of England clergyman who became famous for his translations of the New Testament into accessible, modern English. He was a canon of Salisbury Cathedral from 1964. 14

Pope St Pius X (1835–1914) came from a poor Italian family but quickly rose in eminence to be elected Pope in 1903. He encouraged daily Communion, opposed 'modernism' and was known for his personal holiness. 84

Pliny the Elder (23–79) was a Roman official and writer, remembered for his interest in natural history. He was killed while watching an eruption of Mount Vesuvius. 55

Mary Pettibone Poole was writing for the *Ladies Home Journal* in 1941. 67

Alexander Pope (1688–1744), an English satirical poet and Roman Catholic, he achieved fame with his translations of Homer. He had a great talent for making enemies and an equally great one for making friends. 64, 79

Gerald Priestland (1927–91) was a Quaker and a broadcaster, serving as the BBC's religious correspondent from 1977 to 1982. 6, 31

John Boynton Priestley (1894–1984), a Yorkshire-born prolific playwright, novelist, essayist and broadcaster who commentated on social issues with wit, insight and a true concern. 7

Richard C. Raines was the Methodist Bishop of Indiana from 1948 to 1968. 23

Michael Ramsey (1904–88), an academic and churchman who was Archbishop of Canterbury from 1961 to 1974. During this period, he worked for church unity and became the first English archbishop to visit the Pope since the Reformation. 29, 53, 66

E. C. Ratcliff was a twentieth-century Anglican priest, liturgical scholar and Regius Professor of Theology at Cambridge. 35

Paul S. Rees 20

Joseph Ernest Renan (1823–92) was a French historian and theologian who left the Church but later wrote a controversial life of Jesus. 1

Sir Cliff Richard (1940–) who was born Harry Roger Webb in Lucknow in India is an English pop singer and committed Christian. 10, 13, 39, 80

Johann Paul Richter (1763–1825), often known simply as 'Jean Paul', was a German novelist, humorist and student of theology who satirized both human folly and what he saw as absurd social customs. 10, 36, 38, 54, 65

Oscar Romero (1917–80) lived and worked in his native El Salvador, being priested in 1942 and becoming Archbishop in 1977. He defended the poor, worked for justice and human rights, opposed his country's leaders and made some enemies in Rome. He was murdered while celebrating Mass. 12, 50

Franklin Delano Roosevelt (1882–1945), the only President of the United States of America to be elected four times, he led his country out of the Great Depression and during the Second World War. 3, 50, 57

Theodore Roosevelt (1858–1919), the youngest man ever to become President of the United States of America, he was known as 'Teddy' and gave his name to the teddy bear. 19, 34, 48, 72

Eugen Rosenstock-Huessy (1888–1973) was born Eugen Rosenstock in Berlin, became a lecturer and fought in the First World War. In 1914, he married Margit Huessy, subsequently taking her name and moving to the United States where he became an influential writer and lecturer. 8, 52

Jean Jacques Rousseau (1712–78) was a French writer and philosopher, credited with starting the Romantic Movement. He often wrote about his concept of 'the noble savage': men are naturally free, equal and good – but corrupted by institutions. 17

John Ruskin (1819–1900), an English author and art critic, he was much concerned with the relationship between art, morality and social justice. 9, 22, 35, 90, 91

Bertrand Arthur William Russell (1872–1970) was an English philosopher and mathematician with often unorthodox views. He championed sexual freedom, nuclear disarmament and progressive education – but definitely not Christianity. 2, 37, 64

Antoine Marie Roger de Saint-Exupéry (1900–44) became a pilot in 1926 and wrote about flying in several of his books, which included his children's story *The Little Prince*. Despite his age, he flew for the French Air Force during the Second World War. 51

Carl Sandburg (1878–1967) was an American poet and collector of folk songs who also wrote a major biography of Abraham Lincoln. 49

William Edwyn Sangster (1900–60) was a Methodist preacher, author and scholar. 44, 48, 81

Jean-Paul Sartre (1905–80) was a French existentialist philosopher, dramatist and novelist. 44

Cicely Mary Strode Saunders (1918–) was a pioneer of the hospice movement in England and was created Dame in 1980. 64

Dorothy L. Sayers (1893–1957) was one of the first women graduates from Oxford University. She wrote a number of theological works and a series of radio plays about Jesus (*The Man Born to be King* 1941–2) but is more popularly known for her detective stories featuring Lord Peter Wimsey. 11, 27, 28

Johann Christoph Friedrich von Schiller (1759–1805) was a German poet and dramatist. A friend of Goethe, he also wrote a number of essays. 45

Arthur Schopenhauer (1788–1860) taught that God, free will and the immortality of the soul are all illusions but this German philosopher also argued that chastity is important and that sympathy is even more important. 45

Albert Schweitzer (1875–1965) was a brilliant organist and university lecturer who gave up this work to qualify as a doctor and to work as a missionary in French Equatorial Africa where he established a hospital and leper colony. 42, 48, 62, 68

Peter Selby (1941–), an English theologian, became Bishop of Worcester in 1997. 32, 37

George Bernard Shaw (1856–1950) moved from Ireland to London at the age of 20 and developed a career as a writer, penning a large number of successful plays including *St Joan* and *Pygmalion* (on which *My Fair Lady* is based). He was an outspoken critic of all he thought unfair or silly. 6, 11, 32, 34, 35, 37, 49, 51, 54, 57, 59, 60, 61, 63, 66

Staretz Silouan (1866–1938) was a Russian Orthodox monk. 15

Logan Pearsall Smith (1865–1946) was born in Pennsylvania but spent much of his life in England studying and writing about the English language. 33, 37

Mary F. Smith 80

Sydney Smith (1771–1845) was an English priest renowned for his wit and preaching. 23, 56, 91

Socrates (*circa* 469–399 BC), a Greek philosopher who was indifferent to personal comfort, he did not teach 'a truth' but led his followers and pupils to search for the truth. 24

Benedict de Spinoza (1632–77) was a Dutch philosopher of Jewish parentage. He believed not in a personal God but in a God who is identical with nature. 7

Adlai Ewing Stevenson (1900–65), an American politician, was born in Los Angeles, served under F. D. Roosevelt, failed to win the presidency in 1952 and 1956 and was known for his integrity. 34

Robert Louis Stevenson (1850–94) was born in Edinburgh, travelled widely and finally settled in Samoa. He is now chiefly famous for his children's novels *Treasure Island* and *Kidnapped*. 47, 51, 74

Mary Danvers Stocks (1891–1975) was principal of Westfield College in London and an advocate of women's suffrage and the welfare state. Widely known as a broadcaster, she was later created Baroness. 77

Tom Stoppard (1937–) is a Czech-born English dramatist who has been described as a verbal gymnast and intellectual showman. He is noted for the wit, intellectualism and theatricality of his plays. 1

John Robert Walmsley Stott (1921–) is one of the Church of England's leading evangelical ministers, first becoming well known as a preacher in the London district of Marylebone in the post-war years. He is especially noted for his connection with All Souls' Church in London's Langham Place. 12, 15, 27, 29

Geoffrey Ankestell Studdert-Kennedy (1883–1929) was an English Army chaplain during the First World War, nicknamed 'Woodbine Willie' by soldiers at the Front. After the war, he was a rector in London and wrote several popular religious books. 11, 29

Jonathan Swift (1667–1745), best known as the author of *Gulliver's Travels*, was Dean of St Patrick's Cathedral in Dublin. 16, 36, 63, 65, 70, 90

Alan John Percivale Taylor (1906–90) was an English historian, academic and popular television pundit. 65

Jeremy Taylor (1613–67) was ordained at the age of 20, was made a Doctor of Divinity by royal decree, served as a chaplain to the Royalist army and (after a period of retirement in Wales during the Commonwealth) was made Bishop of Down and Connor just after the Restoration. 4, 36, 72, 92

William Temple (1881–1944) was the son of an Archbishop of Canterbury who himself was elevated to that position in 1942 – having been an Oxford lecturer, a public school headmaster, a London vicar and Archbishop of York, as well as being a prolific writer. 2, 8, 20, 30, 31, 82, 92

St Teresa of Avila (1515–82) was a Spanish Carmelite nun who founded several 'primitive' houses for both monks and nuns, was also a mystic and is remembered for her writings on the various types of prayer from meditation to mystic experience. 18, 22, 44, 56, 59, 63, 79, 81

Mother Teresa of Calcutta (1910–97) was born of Albanian parents in former Yugoslavia, joined an order of nuns and was sent to work in India where she became the founder of the Sisters of Charity, running schools for the poorest children in Calcutta and, later, her Home for the Dying. 18, 55, 79, 80

Quintus Septimus Tertullian (*circa* 155–225) was a convert to Christianity who became a leader of the Church in Africa and wrote a number of theological works. 5, 7, 11, 25, 31, 40, 58, 85

William Makepeace Thackeray (1811–63) was born in Calcutta to English parents. He was a prolific satirical journalist (writing for *Punch* among other periodicals) and novelist – his most famous being *Vanity Fair*. 42, 53

Hilda Margaret Thatcher (1928–) was born in Grantham, Lincolnshire, the daughter of a Methodist grocer. She became a prominent Conservative MP and was the first woman to become a British Prime Minister. 15

St Thomas Aquinas (1225–74) was first a Benedictine and later a Dominican monk who became a university lecturer. A genuinely patient and humble man, his writings also helped establish the Catholic teachings that contraception and abortion are wrong. 7, 9, 12, 16, 22, 27, 28, 49, 74, 84, 85

Gwyn Thomas (1913–81) was a Welsh schoolmaster turned writer, dramatist and broadcaster who wrote about life in the Welsh valleys with wit and humour. 89

Francis Thompson (1859–1907), an English Roman Catholic, gave up training for the priesthood and subsequently for medicine in order to concentrate on writing poetry. 1, 39

Henry David Thoreau (1817–62) wrote the American classic, *Walden*, based on a two-year retreat in a cabin he had built himself. *Walden* reveals his own idealistic faith. 3, 4, 44, 46, 67, 69

Paul Tillich (1886–1965) was a German-born Lutheran pastor who served as a chaplain in the First World War but whose opposition to Naziism led to his emigrating to the United States in 1933. His extensive writing encompasses both popular and academic theology. 41, 44, 75

Leo Nikolaevich Tolstoy (1828–1910) was born into one of Russia's famous noble families, fought in the Crimean War and then travelled widely. One of the world's greatest writers, his two most famous novels are *War and Peace* and *Anna Karenina*. 48, 55

Thomas Traherne (1637–74) was an English Anglican cleric who published one book in his lifetime. His poems, which were not discovered and published until 1903, show considerable originality of thought. 24, 28, 41

Harry S. Truman (1884–1972) fought in the First World War, studied law and then entered politics. He succeeded to the presidency of the United States on Roosevelt's death in 1945 and ordered the dropping of the first atomic bomb. The 'S' in his name represents the names of his grandfathers: it does not stand for any one name. 54

Desmond Mpilo Tutu (1931–), an Anglican priest and an outspoken critic of the apartheid system in his native South Africa, he was awarded the Nobel Peace Prize in 1984 and became Archbishop of Cape Town in 1986. Later he chaired the South African Peace and Reconciliation Commission. 58, 73

Mark Twain is the pen name of **Samuel Langhorne Clemens** (1835–1910), the American novelist now chiefly remembered for his novels *The Adventures of Tom Sawyer* and *The Adventures of Huckleberry Finn*. 36, 37, 90

Kenneth Peacock Tynan (1927–80) was an influential and sometimes controversial British theatre critic and was later literary adviser to the National Theatre. 63

Paul Valéry (1871–1945), a French poet and writer who was also a philosopher and student of mathematics. 67

Gerald Vann (1906–63) was a Roman Catholic priest and author. 74

Marquis de Vauvenargues, otherwise **Luc de Clapiers** (1715–47), was a French soldier who turned to literature. He was a moralist and essayist with a strong belief in the individual's capacity for goodness. 51

Innocent Veniaminov (1797–1879) was the first Russian Orthodox bishop to preach on the American continent. 14, 15

Stephen Edmund Verney (1919–) became an assistant bishop in the Anglican Diocese of Oxford in 1991. 80

St Vincent de Paul (*circa* 1580–1660) was captured by pirates in 1605 and spent two years as a slave in Tunisia. A priest and philosopher, he established a missionary order to work among French peasants; the more famous Sisters of Charity. His life of service to the poor is continued by the lay Society of St Vincent de Paul, established in 1833. 71, 75

Voltaire, otherwise **François Marie Arouet** (1694–1778), was a prolific French writer, producing a succession of histories, satires, plays, verse and philosophy. He condemned all dogmatic religions but was also a tolerant man: 'I may disapprove of what you say but I will defend to the death your right to say it.' 7, 18, 37, 78

Peter de Vries (1910–93) was an American humorous writer and satirist who contributed articles to the *New Yorker* as well as writing several novels including *Brotherhood of the Lamb*, which deals with his daughter's leukemia. 8, 16

George Walden 35

George Washington (1732–99) was the General who defeated the British in the War of Independence and, despite his own wishes, was elected the first President of the United States. 44, 49

Keith Spencer Waterhouse (1929–) is an English journalist, columnist and prolific writer of plays, screenplays and novels. 78

Isaac Watts (1674–1748) was an English independent minister, hymn writer and teacher. His hymns include 'When I survey the wondrous cross' and 'O God, our help in ages past'. 57

Arthur Wellesley, Duke of Wellington (1769–1852), born in Dublin, joined the British army at the age of 18, rising to the rank of General. Made a duke for his successes against Napoleon in Spain and Portugal, he again successfully led the British against him at the Battle of Waterloo (1815). He was Prime Minister from 1828 to 1830. 82

Carolyn Wells (1869–1942) was an American writer of crime fiction. 79

Herbert George Wells (1866–1946) was an English novelist, many of whose works feature the lower middle class in which he grew up. He also wrote science fiction, such as *The Time Machine* and *The War of the Worlds*. 38

John Wesley (1703–91) was an Anglican priest and evangelist who became the founder of the Methodist movement. He usually preached outdoors, travelling some 8,000 miles a year on horseback. Although he wanted Methodism to remain part of Anglicanism, based on a body of lay preachers, it separated by 1784. 32, 48, 58, 81

Susanna Wesley (1669–1742) was the mother of John and Charles Wesley. 32

Mae West (1892–1980) was a voluptuous American screen actress who specialized in glamorous but earthy roles. 76

Edith Newbold Jones Wharton (1862–1937) was an American novelist. Influenced by Henry James, she wrote with wit and irony on ethical and moral themes. 67

Katharine Spencer Whitehorn (1928–), was born in London and became a noted journalist on the Sunday paper, the *Observer* (1960–96). 92

Ralph Wightman (1901–71), was a BBC broadcaster and countryman, famous for his appearances on the radio programme *Any Questions*. He lived and died in the Devon village of Piddletrenthide. 66

Samuel Wilberforce (1805–73), the third son of William (known for his work against slavery), he founded the first Anglican theological college at Cuddesdon in 1854 while Bishop of Oxford. Later, he was Bishop of Winchester and initiated the revision of the Authorized Version of the Bible in 1870. 21, 33

Oscar Wilde (1854–1900), Irish-born writer and wit, he had a number of theatrical successes, lectured widely in the United States but was imprisoned for homosexual offences. 2, 4, 35, 47, 49, 54, 61, 63, 65, 70, 73, 77

David Wilkerson is a North American minister and founding pastor of Times Square Church in New York. Best known for his early days of ministry to young drug addicts and gang members in Manhattan, the Bronx and Brooklyn as told in *The Cross and the Switchblade*. 13, 32, 54

Charles Williams (1886–1945) was an English writer of religious plays and a novelist, often developing religious themes within the thriller genre. 31

Howard Williams, Christian apologist. 47

Rowan Williams (1950–) was Archbishop of Wales from 1998 until 2002, when he became Archbishop of Canterbury. 21

Thomas Wilson (1663–1755), born in Cheshire, England, he became Bishop of Sodor and Man; wrote a 'Manx Catechism'; and is best remembered for his book *Short Instructions for the Lord's Supper*. 24, 78, 82

Thomas Woodrow Wilson (1856–1924) was elected President of the United States of America in 1912 and worked to lower taxes, end child labour and cut working hours. In 1920 he was awarded a Nobel Peace Prize for his work in setting up the League of Nations (an earlier form of the UN) – even though Congress did not let the USA join. 19

St Francis Xavier (1505–52), the son of a nobleman, he was born in the Basque country of northern Spain. With Ignatius Loyola, he formed the Society of Jesus and, at the request of the King of Portugal, he became a missionary in India. 61